DEVELOPMENT CENTRE STUDIES

CHANGING COMPARATIVE ADVANTAGE IN FOOD AND AGRICULTURE:
LESSONS FROM MEXICO

BY

IRMA ADELMAN

AND

J. EDWARD TAYLOR

DEVELOPMENT CENTRE
OF THE ORGANISATION FOR ECONOMIC CO-OPERATION AND DEVELOPMENT

Pursuant to article 1 of the Convention signed in Paris on 14th December 1960, and which came into force on 30th September 1961, the Organisation for Economic Co-operation and Development (OECD) shall promote policies designed:

- to achieve the highest sustainable economic growth and employment and a rising standard of living in Member countries, while maintaining financial stability, and thus to contribute to the development of the world economy;
- to contribute to sound economic expansion in Member as well as non-member countries in the process of economic development; and
- to contribute to the expansion of world trade on a multilateral, non-discriminatory basis in accordance with international obligations.

The original Member countries of the OECD are Austria, Belgium, Canada, Denmark, France, the Federal Republic of Germany, Greece, Iceland, Ireland, Italy, Luxembourg, the Netherlands, Norway, Portugal, Spain, Sweden, Switzerland, Turkey, the United Kingdom and the United States. The following countries became Members subsequently through accession at the dates indicated hereafter: Japan (28th April 1964), Finland (28th January 1969), Australia (7th June 1971) and New Zealand (29th May 1973).

The Socialist Federal Republic of Yugoslavia takes part in some of the work of the OECD (agreement of 28th October 1961).

The Development Centre of the Organisation for Economic Co-operation and Development was established by decision of the OECD Council on 23rd October 1962.

The purpose of the Centre is to bring together the knowledge and experience available in Member countries of both economic development and the formulation and execution of general economic policies; to adapt such knowledge and experience to the actual needs of countries or regions in the process of development and to put the results at the disposal of the countries by appropriate means.

The Centre has a special and autonomous position within the OECD which enables it to enjoy scientific independence in the execution of its task. Nevertheless, the Centre can draw upon the experience and knowledge available in the OECD in the development field.

Publié en français sous le titre :

L'ÉVOLUTION DES AVANTAGES COMPARATIFS
DANS LE SECTEUR AGRO-ALIMENTAIRE

LEÇONS TIRÉES DU MEXIQUE

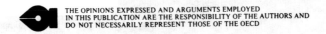

This study forms part of the Development Centre's programme of research on changing comparative advantages in agriculture.

Also available

Development Centre Seminars

ONE WORLD OR SEVERAL? edited by Louis Emmerij (1989)
(41 89 04 1) ISBN 92-64-13249-X 320 pp.   £19.50 US$34.00 FF160 DM66

Development Centre Studies

AGRICULTURAL POLICIES FOR THE 1990s, by Sartaj Aziz (1990)
(41 90 01 1) ISBN 92-64-13350-X 136 pp.   £14.50 US$25.00 FF120 DM47

CHANGING COMPARATIVE ADVANTAGES IN CHINA: Effects on Food,
Feed and Fibre Markets, by Kym Anderson (1990)
(41 90 02 1) ISBN 92-64-13354-2 118 pp.   £15.00 US$25.00 FF120 DM47

OECD ECONOMIC STUDIES (Half–yearly)
ISSN 0255–0830
No. 13/WINTER 1989–1990

Special Issue: MODELLING THE EFFECTS OF AGRICULTURAL POLICIES
(1990)
(13 89 02 1) ISBN 92-64-13329-1 284 pp.
Per issue: £13.50 US$23.50 FF110 DM45
Subscription: £21.00 US$48.00 FF180 DM78

To be published

AGRICULTURE AND ECONOMIC CRISIS: Lessons from Brazil, by Ian Goldin and
Gervasio Castro de Rezende

AGRICULTURAL TRADE LIBERALIZATION: Implications for Developing
Countries, edited by Ian Goldin and Odin Knudsen

Prices charged at the OECD Bookshop.

*The OECD CATALOGUE OF PUBLICATIONS and supplements will be sent free of charge
on request addressed either to OECD Publications Service,
2, rue André-Pascal, 75775 PARIS CEDEX 16, or to the OECD Distributor in your country.*

TABLE OF CONTENTS

I

RETROSPECTIVE ON MEXICAN AGRICULTURAL POLICY AND TRADE, 1950-PRESENT

II

FRAMEWORK OF ANALYSIS

III

FAM MULTIPLIER ANALYSIS

IV

SCENARIO ANALYSIS AND COUNTERFACTUAL EXPERIMENTS

V

CONCLUSION

ACKNOWLEDGEMENTS

We are greatly indebted to Nora Lustig, Antonio Martin del Campo, Antonio Yunez-Naude, Matthew Warning, Alain de Janvry, Manuel Pastor, Jr. and Elias Lopez for their valuable advice and assistance.

PREFACE

The 1986-1988 research programme of the OECD Development Centre has been looking, among other topics, at Changing Comparative Advantages in Food and Agriculture.

The original objectives of this component were:

1. Against a background of technology, population and income trends, how does the future situation of supply and demand of agricultural products look? Are we entering a period of global surpluses or will we continue to witness recurrent phases of serious global deficits?

2. In the light of the OECD countries' declared objective to change their agricultural subsidy policies, what will be the impact of such changes on particular groups of countries in the developing world?

3. The emergence of global surpluses, including export surpluses in some of the bigger developing countries, has not significantly changed the reality of poverty and inadequate food consumption in large parts of the developing world. Analytically, what are the links between global food markets and effective demand for food in poor countries? How far could, and will, a different mix of policy emphasis on "entitlement" and on-farm employment lead to different patterns of demand growth? More generally, how important is it to analyse the different interactions of the various groups within these countries?

4. In terms of the policy implications for OECD Member and non-member countries, what indications can be derived as to rational policy changes which would better help meet the basic needs of the people, give farmers and rural populations a decent living, and produce efficient and stable global markets?

The present study, undertaken by Professor Irma Adelman and Dr. J. Edward Taylor, fits into the third and fourth objectives. It looks at the interaction between alternative agricultural policies in Mexico on the one hand, and the international economic situation on the other. The authors come up with clear conclusions as to which policies would be more beneficially pursued in that country. The analysis suggests that Mexico is better off with a small-farmer based development strategy and an agricultural-led economic development.

The authors have pioneered a quantitative analysis to look at the interactions between agricultural sector policies, the national economy, and the implications of exogenous factors.

Louis Emmerij
President, OECD Development Centre
December 1989

MEXICO: EXECUTIVE SUMMARY

This study is the first in a series of developing country case studies on the interactions between the basic food sector and the rest of the national economy. Other studies are being completed on Argentina and Brazil in Latin America, on Ethiopia and Ghana in sub-Saharan Africa and on China, Pakistan and Thailand in Asia. A parallel study is being undertaken on international interactions in food and agriculture.

In 1987, the Centre initiated a broad programme of research on emerging issues that are of vital interest to both OECD Member and to non-member countries. The aim was to identify issues of growing concern which could be addressed in a preventive rather than a remedial manner. The Centre should draw the contours of these issues, study their implications and suggest policy directions.

The Centre's research on food and agriculture has been guided by three rather distinct concerns. First, how far are current world market conditions for major foodstuffs — characterised by massive surpluses and unremunerative prices — a temporary phenomenon? How far — by contrast — do they reflect a structural disequilibrium? Two opposing trends are in play. On the one hand, income elasticities of demand for food in low income countries remain (or, at least, are potentially) high. Demographic growth rates also remain high, and in some cases (especially China and India) they may be higher than seemed likely a few years ago. Moreover, changing tastes are increasing demand in these countries for internationally traded foods and for livestock products whose cereal and oilseed requirements are much higher than those for diets based on traditional staples.

On the other hand, agriculture in both developed and developing countries has been remarkably successful over the past two decades in adopting yield-increasing technology innovations. Continuing technology innovations suggest that these productivity increases will continue. However, while the potential demand increases will certainly be centered in the low income countries, the technology innovations originate primarily in the developed OECD countries. This suggests that international markets may become increasingly important, and it points to the importance of analysing the insertion of low income countries into these international markets.

The second concern is that it is obvious that international food product markets (and, especially, world prices) are driven at present by OECD country policies. Whatever the conclusions reached about the first concern, the costs of the present situation are becoming unsustainable for the main OECD participants and they are now committed to reducing net protection to their agriculture. What are the implications of plausible OECD policy changes, via international markets, for developing countries? At the same time, many developing countries are in the process of adjusting their own policies for agricultural support. Some of these policy changes might have significant effects on world markets and might be included

9

in international discussions. So, it is relevant to assess the level of "net" protection to (or, discrimination against) agriculture in major developing countries.

The third concern is that, within low income countries, it is important to consider the food consumption (and nutritional status) of different populations. This is important both from a nutritional or poverty standpoint and because national trends in food consumption may be very sensitive to different assumptions about policies affecting different groups of people. An important corollary is that changes in international food product markets interact with national policies to yield different impacts on different population groups within low income countries.

With these preoccupations, the Centre decided to conduct two types of research in parallel. On the one hand, research would be undertaken to analyse the global interactions involving trends in supply, demand and trade, technology, the food system and costs of production in different locations. This would also consider the reciprocal impacts of policy changes in OECD and developing countries, via world markets, on different groups of countries. On the other hand, the Centre would take up individual country case studies for representative and important developing countries, which would analyse the national interactions between food, other agriculture and the rest of the national economy, while taking account of international market trends.

Research has been undertaken for eight developing countries. Initially, studies were carried out on Mexico (presented here) and Pakistan, and these served as a model for later studies. These include: Argentina and Brazil in Latin America, Ethiopia and Ghana in sub-Saharan Africa, and China and Thailand in Asia. Countries were selected both for their importance in relation to the issues, their geographical representativeness and the scope for conducting serious empirical research.

The issues raised in the country case studies reflect the specificities of the different countries, and the research methodologies vary. Nevertheless, they share a common concern with interactions between shorter- and longer-term trends, and between basic food production and consumption and the rest of the national economy. The shorter-term trends include the effects of the economic recession of the past decade and the consequent structural adjustment and policy reactions. The longer-term trends include underlying policies on land tenure, income distribution and public investment in infrastructure and human resources, and the effects of technology change. The country case studies also consider how production and consumption of basic food has been influenced by developments within the national economy and by government policies. At the same time, the studies are all situated against a background of changing international markets for major agricultural products, and, in the Mexican case, with alternative petroleum prices.

Mexico's agricultural development over the past three decades can be characterised in term of successive phases of development strategy. However, Mexican development strategy has never focussed primarily on agriculture. The authors of the present study identify three periods: traditional import-substitution industrialisation (1950-70), foreign-debt and petroleum-export led industrialisation (1970-81) and crisis and austerity (since 1981).

During the first period, there was limited emphasis on agriculture. In effect, there emerged a bimodal policy approach which successfully promoted large-scale agriculture, at the expense of small-farmer agriculture based on maize and beans. During this period, the effects of the Green Revolution, primarily in wheat, are evident in rapid increases in productivity and temporary trade surpluses in basic grains.

The second period, broadly the 1970s, initially continued the bimodal approach, although the emphasis shifted from basic food crops to sorghum as feedstuff for rapidly growing livestock production. This "Second Agricultural Revolution" was bimodal primarily on the consumption side: smaller farmers shared in the benefits of the introduction of high-yielding sorghum, but the resulting livestock products were primarily consumed by the affluent. Mexico shifted towards importing basic foodgrains, while income distribution shifted yet further against the poor.

In the second half of the 1970s, the oil boom and Mexico's associated unrealistic debt aspirations encouraged much more permissive public spending. Although agriculture was not the major beneficiary, there was a short-lived experiment with unimodal growth in 1980-82, directed, on the one hand, at increasing food output gains from small farms (through massive public investment), and, on the other hand, at improving the nutrition of the poor (involving large consumer price subsidies). There were large short-term gains in maize production.

The collapse of petroleum prices in 1981 triggered the subsequent period of crisis and austerity. Mexico returned to a basic foodgrain production towards sorghum and livestock production.

So, somewhat to our initial surprise (since Mexico is a relatively wealthy country not normally associated with food or agricultural trade problems), the country presents a very interesting case for the analysis of the economic interactions which translate our policy concerns.

First, Mexico clearly has a nutritional problem — poor people with insufficient calories — and this has persisted in spite of a relatively high level and rapid growth in per capita incomes and in spite of a decade of plentiful government revenues. The nutritional problem is a reflection of agricultural and income distribution policies which have (with one fitful exception) systematically favoured larger farmers and more affluent consumers.

Second, technology has clearly worked. However, it has primarily worked in favour of wheat and sorghum and, most important, it has been increasingly driven by a livestock revolution which corresponds to affluent demands.

Third, the livestock revolution is outpacing Mexico's capacity to produce feedgrain inputs. The country has shifted from being a (small) net exporter of basic foodstuffs to being one of the world's most important importers of animal feed. This import dependence has survived the 1980s debt crisis.

What might be the outcome in a changed international economic environment or with different domestic political priorities? This is the focus of the present study.

It is clear that with these preoccupations the scope of the study must be both broad and complex. It must also be quantitative. To be able to analyse the nutritional and poverty issues, the authors develop an innovative quantitative framework — a "food accounting matrix" or FAM — using the principles and techniques of social accounting. This FAM is linked to an agricultural and macro-economic model which takes account of longer-term trends: its time-horizon is somewhere in the mid-1990s.

With this modelling framework and a set of "base case" projections which correspond to present bimodal agricultural policies, the analysis tries to pose several "what if" questions, leading to different scenarios and different sets of quantitative results. Three alternative "policy" strategies are considered:

— A *unimodal* strategy, which emphasizes the growth of a productive peasant agriculture and reduces the traditional bias in favour of commercial farming;

— A *populist* strategy for urban sectors, with high wages and high food subsidies;

— A *wage-repression* strategy, essentially based on current post-crisis policies.

Each policy strategy is considered in relation to alternative international macro-economic assumptions, represented by the international prices of petroleum and of food products. The results are presented in terms of nutrition (calorie intakes), agriculture (quantities of different products produced) and macro-economic indicators (income levels, income distribution, government budgets and foreign trade).

The results presented below are both controversial and important. They suggest clearly that the "unimodal" peasant-oriented strategy, which was only adopted when petro-dollars and international debt seemed assured and was abandoned as soon as the boom collapsed, would in fact be the best option for Mexico in its present predicament. In the welfare economist's words, it would be "Pareto-optimal" or a "positive-sum game": every important group in society would be better off and everyone would be better fed than with the alternative strategies.

This result, surprising but greatly reassuring, is very strongly linked to Mexico's balance of payments problems and to trends in consumption of livestock products. Essentially, a shift in agricultural (and, implicitly, income distribution) policies would lead to a massive fall in imports of agricultural products, simultaneously directly benefiting small farmers and indirectly relieving the macro-economic balance of payments constraint on economic development.

This is not simply a question of "structural adjustment with a human face". The longer-term analysis suggests that Mexico must be better off, in terms of all the important economic and social indicators, with a small-farmer based development strategy. The superiority of the "unimodal" strategy is unaffected by radically alternative assumptions about international petroleum or food prices, which are the prices most relevant to Mexico's international problems.

How far can we generalise these results? In analytical terms the results seem rather robust, and the general conclusions are consistent with those of other authors. They strongly reinforce the idea that basic food agriculture and associated activities should be the driving force for economic development even within relatively advanced and industrialised developing countries. Even for a resource-rich country, such as Mexico, and even in the present difficult circumstances, the best way forward is through a peasant-agriculture led economic development.

Whatever the ultimate conclusions on the broad questions for Mexico, the study has justified the Centre's interest in the issues outlined above. More positively, it has developed a quantitative framework for analysing these questions which is both original and at the same time offers very rich potential for future application.

I

RETROSPECTIVE ON MEXICAN AGRICULTURAL POLICY AND TRADE 1950-PRESENT

The overriding thrust of Mexican economic development policy since the 1950s has been on industry-led growth (a process referred to as "developmentalism"), with a primary focus on import-substitution industrialization. On the industrial side, this process has been supported by imports of intermediate inputs and capital goods; the primary constraint on industrial growth has been the availability of foreign exchange to finance imports of manufactured inputs, capital goods, and after the 1960s, food to support rapid urbanization. On the agricultural side, Mexico has followed a classic bi-modal development strategy, with the exception of a brief experiment in unimodal agricultural growth in the late 1970s and early 1980s. Development policy actively has supported comercial farms to generate foreign exchange and to provide food for domestic consumption. Meanwhile, growth in agricultural productivity on small farms, where the vast majority of the rural farm population resides, has lagged behind that of commercial farms.

One can distinguish three periods with regard to the interactions between Mexico's macro-economic constraints and general policy thrust, on the one hand, and its patterns of agricultural development and agricultural trade, on the other: traditional import-substitution industrialization (1950-1970), foreign-debt and petroleum-export led industrialization (1970-1981) and crisis and austerity (1981 to present).

I.1.TRADITIONAL IMPORT-SUBSTITUTION LED INDUSTRIAL GROWTH (1950-1970)

This period was marked by the usual import-substitution policies of industrialization behind heavy tariff walls. It was a period of transition from reliance on imported consumer goods to a reliance on imported capital goods and intermediate inputs for local production first, of consumer goods, then progressively capital and intermediate goods. The industrialization was financed by heavy foreign investment. Large food surpluses, protectionism and peso over-valuation led to rapid rates of real industrial growth - 5.7 per cent from 1950 to 1970. The share of industry in GDP rose steadily, from 22.7 per cent in 1950 to 29.1 per cent in 1970.

In agriculture, the beginning of the period saw a retreat from the small-farmer, *ejido*-oriented agricultural strategy of the mid-1930s towards an agricultural strategy stressing increased production of wheat on commercial farms. This strategy involved a bimodal approach to agricultural development. It entailed research, input subsidies, and infrastructural investment directed at a commercial farming sector producing food for middle-income urban Mexicans and for agricultural exports, combined with neglect of the ejido-reform sector. High-value vegetable truck farming in the northern border areas and agricultural processing for export to the United States were initiated. The commercial wheat farms underwent a Green Revolution (also referred to as "The First Agricultural Revolution") in the 1950s and 1960s, in which the dwarf wheat varieties were first introduced and yields more than tripled, to 3.02 metric tons per hectare in 1970 (Figure 1). The agricultural strategy was intended to stabilize the overall development effort. It was marked by growing capitalization in agriculture. Total cropland increased 16 per cent between 1950 and 1970, but the land area in irrigation, which is concentrated in the large-farm regions of the North and Northwest, rose 71 per cent during this period; as a result, the share of irrigated cropland increased sharply (Figure 2). This was accompanied by a significant increase in fertilizer use, from 1.09 to 23.21 kilograms per hectare, and in tractors per hectare, from 1.14 to 3.91 (Figures 3a-b). In the early 1960s, Mexico became a food surplus country and a net exporter of basic grains (Figure 4). From 1964 to 1969, Mexico's trade surplus in corn, wheat and beans averaged 10.5 per cent of the country's total production volume in these commodities.

Despite a 29.2 per cent decline in the real government guaranteed price of wheat during this period, wheat production was very profitable, due to input subsidies and use of modern inputs on commercial farms; the latter are illustrated in Figure 1 by dramatic increases in wheat yields. However, government policies also maintained low real prices for maize and beans, the food staples produced on small farms for consumption by the lower income groups. Measured in real terms, the government guaranteed prices of maize and beans fell 16.8 per cent and 17.4 per cent, respectively, between 1960 and 1970. As a result, commercial production of these commodities was relatively unprofitable for all but modern input-intensive farms that succeeded in securing sufficient government support (inputs and credit) to countervail the adverse terms of trade. As real product prices fell and yields on commercial farms increased, the ratio of agricultural input prices to product prices fell 16 per cent from 1960 to 1970. The effect of these agricultural policies was to provide low-price food for the cities; to deteriorate the distribution of income in the rural economy; and to generate dualistic output growth in different farm products: a green-revolution in wheat, coupled with relatively slow growth in corn and beans[1].

I.2. FOREIGN-DEBT AND PETROL-EXPORT DRIVEN IMPORT-SUBSTITUTION DEVELOPMENT (1970-1981)

I.2.1. Pre-Oil Boom

By the late 1960s, the limits to import substitution industrialization started becoming apparent given its structural dependence on foreign capital and imports. The success of Mexican industry in expanding production into intermediate and capital goods sectors was limited. There was a growing reliance on imports in the industrial sector. Protectionism had fostered an increasingly uncompetitive production structure in industry. While rapid industrialization continued behind heavy tariff walls (Figure 5), it began to occur at the

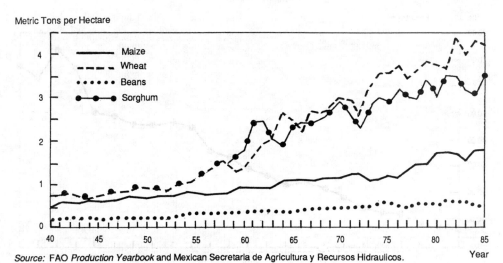

Figure 1. **YIELDS OF SELECTED GRAINS, MEXICO**
1940 - 1985

Metric Tons per Hectare

Maize
Wheat
Beans
Sorghum

Year

Source: FAO *Production Yearbook* and Mexican Secretaria de Agricultura y Recursos Hidraulicos.

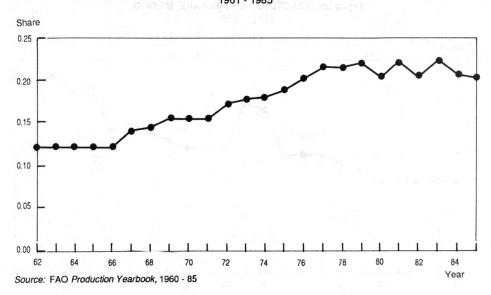

Figure 2. **SHARE OF TOTAL CROPLAND IN IRRIGATION**
1961 - 1985

Share

Year

Source: FAO *Production Yearbook*, 1960 - 85

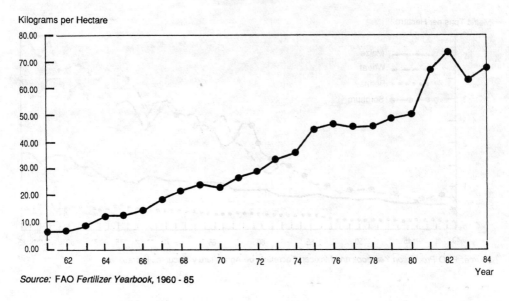

Figure 3a. **MEXICAN FERTILIZER CONSUMPTION PER HECTARE**
1960 - 1984

Kilograms per Hectare

Source: FAO *Fertilizer Yearbook*, 1960 - 85

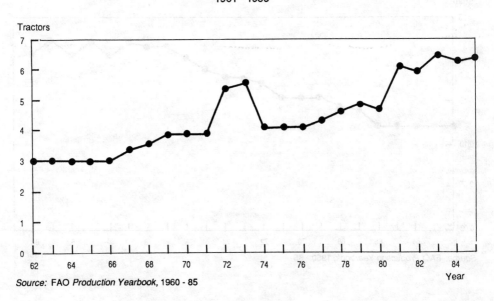

Figure 3b. **TRACTORS PER HECTARE, MEXICO**
1961 - 1985

Tractors

Source: FAO *Production Yearbook*, 1960 - 85

16

expense of agricultural development. The gains in agricultural output from the First Agricultural Revolution had begun to run their course. Basic grains production, which increased 5.35 per cent annually from 1950 to 1969, stagnated from 1970 to 1979, during a period of high population growth in Mexico. Mexico became a net importer of agricultural commodities (Figure 4). In volume terms, Mexican maize imports averaged 18.6 per cent of total maize production between 1973 and 1981. Large trade deficits are also evident for wheat; these reached one-third to more than one-half of the volume of total wheat production in 1979-1981. For the first time in a decade, trade deficits in beans appeared in 1974, 1975 and 1980.

Increasingly large imports of all three foodgrains in the 1970s were due in part to the rapid growth in urban demand coupled with a decrease in productivity growth in basic food crops under Mexico's bimodal growth strategy. They were also fueled by a shift in cropping patterns towards sorghum, to be used as livestock feed. In the late 1960s, the hybrid sorghum, developed in Texas, diffused very rapidly into Mexico, replacing food crops, in what some call the Second Green Revolution (DeWalt, 1985). Average sorghum yields increased 98 per cent from 1960 to 1981 to 3.56 tons per hectare. In absolute terms, the expansion of acreage in sorghum production was three times the total expansion in cropland from 1970 to 1981, and the share of sorghum area in total crop area grew from 3.97 per cent to 7.54 per cent in this period. By 1981, the area in sorghum equalled more than one-fifth the area in maize, four-fifths the area in beans and twice the area in wheat.

Government price policies appear to have favoured production of sorghum relative to basic food crops. The ratio of the average rural Mexican price to the world price of sorghum fell 3.8 per cent from 1970 to 1977, compared to 24.8 per cent for maize and 23.1 per cent for wheat. Sorghum production has been attractive to many commercial farmers because of its low labour requirement (it has just 39 per cent of the average perhectare labour requirement of maize), its high profitability and also its resilience to drought, which makes it a relatively low-risk crop for rainfed lands. Nevertheless, in 1977, 30 per cent of sorghum acreage was in irrigation, compared to 7 per cent for maize and 4.6 per cent for beans. As a result of the large input demand for feedgrains and the deteriorating terms of trade for foodgrains, Mexico's per capita production of food staples never again reached the levels of the mid-1960s.

The Second Agricultural Revolution was a continuation of Mexico's dualistic agricultural strategy, even though sorghum was produced in small mechanized farms with modern technology rather than, like wheat, in large farms, and it did not require irrigated land. The dualism of the Second Agricultural Revolution is in its consumption effects: it promoted livestock production for the benefit of the affluent, whose meat consumption was high, while importing cheap food for the masses. Percapita foodgrain production was lower in 1981 than in 1970, but the deficit in foodgrains was made up by imports. However, there was a large drop in the income share of the poorer income groups in Mexico in the 1970s. This unequal distribution of income was reflected in a severe maldistribution of food (INN).

Continuation of Mexico's industrialization strategy without making major structural changes in the economy required borrowing outside capital. The major outward symptom of a structural economic malaise in the early 1970s was a growing foreign debt: in 1970 Mexico's external public debt equalled 9.7 per cent of GNP; in 1977 it stood at 26.5 per cent of GNP despite record oil exports, and Mexico's interest payments on the external public debt absorbed over 30 per cent of total export revenue (World Bank).

17

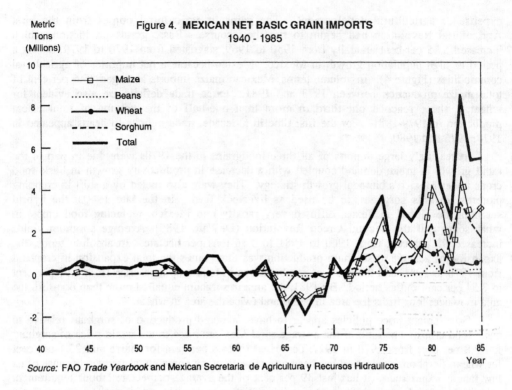

Metric Tons (Millions)

Figure 4. **MEXICAN NET BASIC GRAIN IMPORTS**
1940 - 1985

Legend:
— Maize
.... Beans
— Wheat
- - - Sorghum
— Total

Year

Source: FAO *Trade Yearbook* and Mexican Secretaria de Agricultura y Recursos Hidraulicos

Figure 5. **SECTORAL GROWTH OF MEXICAN ECONOMY**
1970 - 1984

Millions of 1970 Pesos

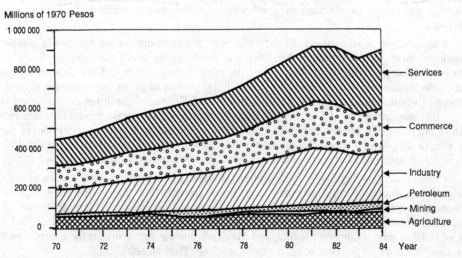

Services
Commerce
Industry
Petroleum
Mining
Agriculture

Year

Source: Mexican Instituto Nacional de Estadistica, Geografia e Informacion (INEGI)
and Economic Commission for Latin America (ECLA)

18

I.2.2. The Oil Boom (1976-1981)

In 1976 there was a doubling of proven oil reserves and a doubling of oil exports in one year. The heart of the economic development strategy under the first half of the Portillo administration was "to convert oil into wealth-generating renewable and technologically structured resources." The period 1976-1981 was characterized by heavy foreign borrowing against oil reserves, continued overvaluation of the peso, and (alas) an escalation of corruption in government.

On the agricultural side, with the federal budget buoyed by petroleum revenues, there was a short-lived experiment with unimodal growth in 1980-1982 with the implementation of the Systema Alimentario Mexicano (SAM). The SAM programme aimed, on the production side, at achieving food output gains from small farms, and on the consumption side, at increasing the caloric intake of the poorest segments of the Mexican population. This entailed a large infusion of government investment into small-scale agriculture and large price subsidies to consumers of basic grains. On the production side the immediate results were impressive. Acreage planted in maize, beans and wheat averaged 9.68 million hectares in 1980-82 — 9 per cent higher than in the previous three years. Total output of these basic grains reached an all-time high of 17 million tons in 1980-82 — 29.9 per cent above the average 1977-79 level. The self-sufficiency targets of the SAM programme were in fact surpassed in 1981, and maize imports plunged from a high of 3.2 million tons in 1980 (to cover the 1979 production shortfall) to 1.2 million tons in 1982. Basic grain imports relative to production decreased from a high of 37 per cent in 1980 to 8 per cent in 1982[2].

The biggest contributor to these increases was a significant rise in productivity, due to an increase of basic grain crops on irrigated lands and greater use of new technological packages in rain-fed areas. The incentives offered by the SAM appear to have been used widely by poor peasants as well as by commercial farmers (Andrade and Blanc, 1987).

Critics argue that the SAM programme's success was at the cost of a growing federal budget deficit resulting from a wedge between basic food prices to farmers and consumers coupled with the large government budget devoted to the SAM programme. Real government input subsidies to the agricultural and livestock sector grew at an average annual rate of 96.6 per cent in 1980-1982, compared to 66.6 per cent in 1978-79. The total government food budget grew at an average annual rate of 50.6 per cent during the three years of the SAM programme compared with 38.3 per cent in 1978-79[3].

These impressive growth rates in government expenditures on food programmes, however, need to be considered in the context of lavish federal spending during the oil boom. The federal food budget actually declined as a per centage of total federal expenditures, from 8.2 per cent to 7.5 per cent, during the first year of the SAM programme. At the 1981 peak of the programme, the food budget rose to 10.8 per cent of the total federal budget, declining to 9.9 per cent in 1982. The incremental cost of the SAM programme has been estimated at US$275 million per year — the equivalent of 1.5 per cent of the Mexican federal budget (Andrade and Blanc, 1987).

I.3. CRISIS AND AUSTERITY, 1981 TO PRESENT

July 3, 1981 witnessed a steep drop in the price of Mexican crude oil and the beginning of what is now commonly referred to as "la crisis." Plummeting oil prices, combined with world-wide recession, rising interest rates in the United States, inefficiencies resulting from protectionism in Mexico, and a shortening of loan repayment schedules challenged the wisdom of following a strategy of import-substitution industrialization financed largely by a single export. In 1982, declining revenues from exports and tourism were not sufficient to cover interest and principal on the nation's $85 billion foreign debt. Massive peso devaluations significantly increased the price of imports, creating serious bottlenecks for industrial production, which depended heavily on imports of capital, technology and other inputs.

The economic crisis triggered an austerity programme which has had major implications for the Mexican agricultural sector. The most immediate of these was the almost complete dismantling of the SAM programme beginning in December 1982 and the return to a bi-modal agricultural development strategy with a continuation of the shift away from production of basic grains for direct human consumption towards production of feedgrains. The area planted in sorghum increased 8.6 per cent between 1980-82 and 1983-85 to 1.8 million hectares. This was nearly twice the growth in basic grains area over this period, which was less than one-half of one per cent. It has been estimated that up to onehalf of Mexico's farmland currently produces grain for livestock (DeWalt, 1985). Nevertheless, a trade deficit in excess of 24 per cent of the total volume of sorghum production persisted throughout the first half of the 1980s. In 1981 Mexico was the second largest importer of sorghum from the United States and the third largest user of the grain in the world.

On the consumption side, despite increases in average per capita meat consumption ranging from 32 per cent for beef to 65 per cent for pork in the 1970s, surveys by the National Nutrition Institute found that meat plays no role whatsoever in the diet of 36 per cent of the Mexican population (INN). This reflects a serious maldistribution of food consumption which is linked to a severe inequality of income and hence, of effective demand for food. Significantly, had Mexico's per capita demand for grain remained constant from 1940 to 1979, the substantial progress in agricultural productivity in Mexico could easily have met the demands of the growing population. Current food shortages are the result of a major shift in the tastes and effective demand of middle and upperclass consumers towards meat consumption, combined with the relative inefficiency of meat in converting grains into calories.

I.4. THE STRUCTURE OF PROTECTION AND MACROECONOMIC REFORM

A macroeconomic reform package adopted in 1985 includes efforts to reduce global economic distortions that have discouraged agricultural and agroindustrial exports and that shifted the internal terms of trade sharply against agriculture during the 1960s and 1970s. Dramatic devaluations of the peso in excess of domestic inflation, together with a large decrease in Mexican real wages in the 1980s, have significantly enhanced the competitiveness of Mexican exports on world markets. The structure of protection in agriculture has varied greatly across sectors and over time. In 1985, the basic-grains sector benefited from a positive rate of protection (16 per cent), while all other agricultural and agro-industrial activities had large negative protection rates — both nominal and effective (see Table 1). The nominal protection rate is the ratio of domestic to world prices in domestic currency (at the official exchange rate), adjusted for transport cost and marketing margins. The effective protection rate measures the total level of protection, including protection through inputs in production. It is calculated using nominal protection rates for 1986 and the Leontief multiplier matrix in our FAM model (See Chapters II and III for a discussion of the multiplier analysis). A negative effective or nominal rate of protection indicates that domestic prices are below world prices. If the rate is positive, as in cereals, the difference between domestic and world prices is maintained through a system of quantitative restrictions on agricultural imports coupled with trading monopolies granted to agricultural parastatals. If the rate is negative, as in all other agricultural and agro-industrial commodities, maintaining domestic prices below world prices involves large subsidies on the output side, the input side, or both. For example, the domestic price of maize, under the 1986 exchange rate, exceeded the world price of corn; however, the price of tortillas to consumers was heavily subsidized and reflected substantial losses in the government milling activities, which resulted in a negative rate of effective protection for maize products and milling on the order of 80 per cent. Negative effective rates of protection also reflect some input subsidies not captured in the input-output matrix, such as subsidized agricultural credit, which equalled 0.6 per cent of GDP in 1985; subsidized production and distribution of improved seeds by government parastatals; subsidized irrigation (a 60 per cent subsidy in 1986), national crop and livestock insurance, and extension and research, estimated at 2.1 per cent of gross agricultural production in 1980. These subsidies overwhelmingly have been targeted at large-scale, commercial agriculture. For example, less than 20 per cent of all low-income agricultural producers receive institutional credit in any given year, and very few small holdings benefit from irrigation and hence, from water subsidies. For the agricultural-related sectors as a whole, the weighted average effective rate of protection was substantially below that of the other sectors in the Mexican economy in the 1980s. This reflects a strong bias in pricing policies against agriculture and agriculture related industries, in the interest of maintaining cheap food, for social reasons and to support industrialization. Most agricultural and agroindustrial production is still under price control, even though the share has fallen since 1985.

The trends in protection in the 1980s, under international pressure, have been to reduce quantitative restrictions on imports and eliminate subsidies for agricultural exports; however, measuring the effects of these policies on protection is difficult, because movements in the nominal protection rates have been dominated by exchange-rate policy (See Table 2). For example, the nominal protection rate for maize has ranged from -32 per cent in 1982, when the exchange rate quadrupled, to 210 per cent in 1978, at the end of a long period of substantial peso overvaluation. There also has been a tendency to replace quantitative restrictions with pricing and tariff policies. As in most countries, in Mexico effective protection rates reflect a political compromise among governmental policy objectives, conflicting rural-urban interest-group pressures, macroeconomic constraints and policies, and international pressures for policy and institutional reform. The result has been very uneven protection and liberalization over time.

There has also been a stated effort since 1985 to reduce farm input subsidies and global food subsidies and to replace these with subsidies aimed at the poor. Finally, the current administration has taken steps to restructure government agricultural institutions, and it has an expressed policy of redirecting public-sector investment toward rainfed areas where small farmers are concentrated and toward small-scale irrigation projects.

The need to reduce cereal imports, which increased 55 per cent between 1974 and 1985, while also reducing the public-sector deficit suggests that output objectives will loom large in Mexican agricultural policy in coming years. Although output objectives are not necessarily inconsistent with the goal of improving the distribution of farm production, a

Table 1. **Nominal and effective rates of agricultural protection for Mexico, 1985**

Per cent

		Rates of protection	
		Nominal[1]	Effective (ERP)[2]
1.	Basic grains	16.00	16.06
2.	Livestock	−37.00	−48.61
3.	Other agricultural	−20.00	−23.17
4.	Petroleum	−50.00	−66.10
5.	Fertilizer	−42.00	−44.90
6.	Agricultural processing	−43.12	−61.38

1. Aggregated from Nominal Protection Rates for October-December 1986 from IMF.
2. Calculated using Nominal Protection Rates and the Leontief multiplier submatrix of the FAM of Table 5.

Table 2. **Nominal protection rates for selected agricultural commodities (percentage) and Mexican exchange rates**

Pesos to dollars, 1978-1985

Years	Maize	Wheat	Sorghum	Coffee rate	Exchange
1970	−4.05	8.15	−58.20	−24.44	12.50
1981	42.62	−15.48	25.70	−28.98	26.23
1982	−32.43	−63.33	−43.80	−68.85	68.85
1983	−9.03	−47.13	−30.70	−59.89	143.93
1984	11.42	−26.26	1.00	−69.27	192.56
1985	7.14	−39.97	−41.30	−70.27	371.70

Source: Calculated from FAO Statistical Yearbook and USDA Commodity Trade Statistics (for world prices); Mexican Secretaria de Agricultura y Recursos Hidraulicos (SARH) (for domestic prices); and IMF Financial Statistics (for exchange rates).

22

substantial shift toward public investment policies favouring small, rainfed farms would .
a significant departure from bimodal agricultural investment policies of the past.

On the demand side, sharp decreases in Mexican real wages do not bode well for efforts to reduce inequality in food consumption in Mexico. Subsidies to poor households can be used to counteract the detrimental effect of falling real wages on the distribution of food consumption. However, the use of such subsidies is likely to be limited by the need to reduce public-sector and foreign-trade deficits.

The agricultural policy of Mexico illustrates well the tradeoffs between production goals and distributional goals within agriculture in particular and the trade and fiscal implications of agricultural policies. It also illustrates rural-urban development tradeoffs and the direct and indirect effects of global development policies on the agricultural sector.

II

FRAMEWORK OF ANALYSIS

In this chapter we present a framework for analyzing Mexico's food economy under alternative development policy and world market scenarios. Specifically, our framework is designed to examine interactions between changing world market conditions and Mexican development policy, on the one hand, with Mexican agricultural production, the distribution of food consumption, and international trade, on the other. in rural and urban areas; and agricultural trade.

II.1. CHANGING WORLD MARKET CONDITIONS

The most critical world-market variable relevant to Mexico is the international price of oil. This defines the foreign exchange constraints on Mexican development policy. Given the direct role of the Mexican state in oil production, it also determines to a great extent the public-sector budget constraint. Finally, variations in world oil prices have an important impact on the exchange rate, and therefore on the competitiveness of Mexican agricultural (and other) exports in foreign markets, the price of food (and other) imports relative to domestically-produced food, and the agricultural terms of trade. Alternative world oil market scenarios are critical to the design of Mexican agricultural development policies and to their impact on the level of food production and on the distribution of food consumption in Mexico. On the distribution side, world market conditions affect wage policy and the capacity of the public sector to pay food subsidies. Thus, they influence the distribution of effective demand for food and the agricultural terms of trade.

II.2. MEXICAN DEVELOPMENT POLICY

Macro policies in Mexico have major direct and indirect impacts on the food sector. The macroeconomic environment in which food production takes place is shaped by price policy (divergence of domestic output prices from world prices due to protection for nonagricultural products and cheap food policies), which affects the agricultural terms of trade; exchange-rate policy, which influences the terms of trade between traded and

24

nontraded goods, including the cost of imported agricultural inputs and the competitiveness of agro-exports; availability of credit, interest-rate policy, and tax policies. In addition to these global policies, sectorspecific policies directly influence the level and distribution of food production. Examples of these include rural development programmes (e.g., the SAM programme), agricultural research and extension, and direct publicsector investment in agriculture. A major focus of our analysis of alternative scenarios is to explore the implications of alternative global and sectoral development policies for the Mexican food economy and the food trade deficit.

II.3. DEMOGRAPHIC TRENDS AND DEMAND PATTERNS

Major demographic trends include urbanization, labour force growth and emigration. Migration of labour out of rural Mexico influences food supplies. Urbanization and trends in the level and distribution of income can be expected to have major impacts on food demand, including consumer tastes. To an important extent, these variables are influenced by development policy as it affects the rural-urban income gap, within-sector income distributions, and education, particularly in rural areas. Population and labour-force growth, changes in world food demand and developed-country trade policies also influence the demand for Mexican farm products.

The effects of alternative world market, development policy and demand scenarios will be explored with respect to both the level and distribution of farm output. The distributional side of the analysis will focus on the distribution of output across land-tenure groups (large commercial farms versus campesino, or small peasant farms, and minifundia, or subsistence farms) and the distribution of output across crops (especially grains for human consumption versus feedgrains).

Disparities in the impacts of Mexican food and agriculture policy across commodities and regions may be due to distributional biases in agricultural research focus (e.g., emphasis on increasing the returns to fertilizer, irrigation, and farm management, which benefit primarily commercial farms, versus developing improved rainfed-crop technology); unequal distribution of extension and inadequate extension service, particularly in the poorest farm regions of Central Mexico; inequality in the distribution of public-sector investments across regions and farmer groups; distribution and administration of farm inputs through parastatal marketing institutions; distribution of access to farm credit; and the distribution of interest-rate and input and price subsidies.

II.4. FOOD ACCOUNTING MATRIX

The objectives cited above call for an analytical framework capable of capturing complex interlinkages between the world economy and Mexican food producers, between food producers and other productive sectors, between production and household incomes in rural and urban areas, and between household incomes and expenditure patterns.

This will be accomplished through the use of a Food Accounting Matrix (FAM). The FAM will serve as a general framework for analyzing the supply and demand for food and other agricultural products in Mexico and the impacts of policy changes and economic trends on output and distribution in the Mexican food economy. The FAM is an accounting tool

25

modeled on the Social Accounting Matrix (Stone, 1985; King, 1981; Pyatt and Round, 1977). It summarizes the destinations (demand) for foodgrains and other agricultural and nonagricultural commodities produced in Mexico and the origins (supply) of these products purchased in Mexico, and it ensures consistency (total supply = total demand) in the Mexican food economy.

Food and other agricultural products are supplied by imports and by a wide variety of farms in Mexico ranging from large commercial farms to small and medium privately owned or ejido farms, mostly on rain-fed lands, to a great number of subsistence or partly self-sufficient private or ejido plots (minifundia). The majority of food producers in Mexico are concentrated in the last two groups. A classification of producers by farm size in the FAM is critical for addressing the distribution of output and output-supply responses across farms. On the expenditure side, it is also essential for addressing basic needs and the distribution of food consumption in the poorest (in terms of landholdings) farm households.

Total demand for food and agricultural products includes the purchase of farm products as inputs by firms inside and outside the farm sector (an important component of this intermediate demand is the purchase of feedgrains by the livestock sector), export demand, and domestic consumption demand by the rural household-farm groups listed above and by urban households. Urban households include households in diverse income groups with varying propensities to spend income on different categories of farm products.

The FAM summarizes the flows of food and other farm products between suppliers and demanders of these goods. More importantly, it ensures consistency when conducting policy analysis and counterfactual experiments on the food economy. For example, if domestic food prices equal world food prices, and if there effectively are no foreign-exchange constraints on food imports, then any increase in the food deficit will be satisfied by international trade, and the FAM will be entirely demand-driven. If domestic food prices are below world food prices (as in the case of Mexico's cheap food policies of the past 3 decades) and there are no federal budget or foreign exchange constraints, the change in the food deficit times the difference between world and domestic prices will show up as a government budget deficit. If the exchange rate is also overvalued, then the food subsidy payment will also show up as a foreignexchange deficit. By contrast, if there is a binding foreign-exchange constraint on food imports (as during the post-oil boom period), an excess demand for food will be filled through a combination of (smaller) food imports, a downward adjustment in food consumption, and some combination of an (upward) adjustment of food prices and an increase in the federal budget deficit (if the federal government intervenes to minimize food price increases). To the extent that both a public-sector budget constraint and a foreign-exchange constraint are binding, more of the world price of food imports will be passed on to food consumers. There is then likely to be a sharper downward adjustment in food consumption, a premium on expanding domestic food production, and an increase in inequality of food consumption. The last scenario most closely reflects the current situation in Mexico. Although price responses cannot be modeled explicitly in the fixed-price, FAM framework, they play a major role in the design and interpretation of our policy experiments.

Three features distinguish our FAM from the conventional Social Accounting Matrix. First, the primary focus of the FAM is on the food economy. Thus, the FAM provides a high level of detail on the food sector, in terms of the distribution of food output by farm size, and on food consumption, in terms of food expenditure patterns of different rural and urban household groups.

A second distinguishing feature of the FAM is that it includes flows of both income and calories. Foodgrain calories are absorbed by the foodgrain sector (as seed), by nonfoodgrain-producing sectors (e.g., livestock), by households for direct human consumption, by government food procurement agencies (e.g., CONASUPO), and by foreigners. These calorie flows are woven into the FAM in a manner analogous to income flows. A major advantage of this approach is that it makes it possible to estimate calorie multipliers to examine the effect of government policies and other exogenous shocks on calorie consumption, and to examine the distribution of calories as well as income across different household groups.

A third novel feature of the FAM is that it does not assume unitary expenditure elasticities on the household consumption and savings side of the economy, thereby relaxing the assumption that marginal budget shares equal average budget shares. This provides a more realistic representation of changes in household expenditure patterns in response to income changes.

II.5. A PROTOTYPE FAM

Table 3 summarizes the basic structure of the FAM for a simple twosector, one-factor economy. Rows and columns corresponding to income flows are denoted by "$;" rows and columns corresponding to calorie flows are denoted by "C." The two productive sectors in this simplified FAM are agriculture and nonagriculture. Intermediate flows of income and of calories between these sectors appear in the interindustry flows matrix in the northwest corner of the FAM. The two rows corresponding to agriculture in this submatrix present, in Columns 1 and 2, flows of income and calories within agriculture (e.g., sales of basic grains as seed and as animal feed), and in Columns 3 and 4, forward income and calorie linkages out of agriculture (e.g., sale of agricultural products to food processors). The first two columns of the interindustry flows submatrix contain, in Rows 3 and 4, backward linkages from agriculture to nonagriculture. Backward calorie linkages from agriculture to nonagriculture are likely to be negligible. Backward income linkages from agriculture to nonagriculture include the purchase of manufactured farm inputs.

Continuing down the columns corresponding to agriculture and nonagriculture, Row 5 presents payments to factors of production, or valueadded. Firms also make payments to government in the form of indirect taxes and profits from state-run industries (Row 8), to foreigners in the form of imports (Row 10), and to a capital account in the form of savings (Row 9). They also import calories (Row 11) and lose calories through wastage (Row 14).

The factor accounts (Column 5) channel value-added into various household groups (Row 6); households in turn use this income to purchase consumer goods, to pay direct taxes to government, and to save (Column 6). Our various household groups also consume calories. Column 7 summarizes the distribution of calorie consumption across households.

Government, in addition to receiving income from direct and indirect taxes, also receives income from the Rest-of-World account through import tariffs (Row 8, Column 10). It channels income into the purchase of goods and services from the two production sectors, production subsidies, transfer payments to households, export subsidies and government savings (Column 8).

Foreigners purchase commodities and calories; they send remittances into the economy (e.g., from migrants working abroad); they pay tariffs, supply savings and provide calories in

Table 3. A simple FAM

	Agricultural		Non-agricultural		Factors	Households		Government		Rest of the world		Capital		Waste	Total	
	1 $	2 C	3 $	4 C	5 $	6 $	7 C	8 $	9 C	10 $	11 C	12 $	13 C	14 C	15 $	16 C
Agriculture 1 $	I-O	0	I-O	0	0	C	0	G	0	E	0	I	0	0	Total $ Prod.	0
2 C	0	CIO	0	CIO	0	0	CC	0	CG	0	CE	0	0	CW	0	Total C Prod.
Non-agriculture 3 $	I-O	0	I-O	0	0	C	0	G	0	E	0	I	0	0	Total $ Prod.	0
4 C	0	CIO	0	CIO	0	0	CC	0	CG	0	CE	0	0	CW	0	Total C Prod.
Factors 5 $	VA	0	VA	0	0	0	0	0	0	0	0	0	0	0	TVA	0
Households 6 $	0	0	0	0	y (Distribution-factor)	0	0	Government transf	0	Remittances	0	0	0	0	THHY	0
7 C	CP (Indirect)	–	CP	–	–	0	0	0	0	0	0	0	0	0	0	THHC
Government 8 $	T (Indirect)	0	T	0	0	T (Direct)	0	0	0	Tariffs	0	0	0	0	TGY	0
9 C	0	CT	0	CT	0	0	0	0	0	0	0	0	0	0	0	TGC
Rest of the world 10 $	$M	0	$M	0	0	0	0	Subsidies	0	0	0	0	0	0	T$M	0
11 C	0	CM	0	CM	0	0	0	0	0	0	0	0	0	0	0	TCM
Capital 12 $	$S	0	$S	0	0	S	0	GS	0	FS	0	II	0	0	T$S	0
13 C	0	CS	0	CS	0	0	0	0	GCS	0	Food aid	0	CII	0	0	TCS
Wastage calories 14 C	0	CW	0	CW	0	0	0	0	0	0	0	0	0	0	0	TW
Total $ 15	TOTAL EXPENDITURE															
Total C 16																

Rows + columns: $ = Income flows; C = Calorie flows.

Key: I-O: Leontief Input-Output Account; CI-O: Calorie Input-Output Account; C, G, E, and I: Consumption, Government, Export, and Investment Demand, respectively; CC, CG, CE: Consumption, Government, and Export Demand for Calories, respectively; CW: Calorie Wastage; VA: Value-Added; CP: Calorie Payment to Households; T and CT: taxes and calorie taxes, respectively; M(CM): Imports (Imports of Calories); S, GS, FS, and CS: Household, Government, Foreign and investment, respectively; THHY (THHC): Total Household Income (Calories); TM (TCM): Total Imports (Calorie Imports); TS (TCS): Total Savings (Calorie Savings); TGY (TGC): Total Government Income (Calories); TW: Total Wastage.

the form of food aid (Columns 10 and 11). The capital account takes total savings and channels them into demand for investment goods (Column 12). Part of the calorie production is absorbed as wastage (Column 14).

II.6. PRODUCTION ACCOUNTS AND INSTITUTIONS IN THE FINAL FAM

In the final FAM, the production side is expanded to nine sectors and the institution side is expanded to include seven household groups. The accounts in the final FAM are summarized in Table 4. The production side includes three agricultural production sectors (foodgrain agriculture, livestock, and other (food plus nonfood) agriculture), a food-processing sector, petroleum, fertilizer, other industries, services and commerce. The principal rationale for this combination of production accounts is to highlight (1) foodgrain agriculture, (2) interactions between foodgrain agriculture, nonfoodgrain agriculture and the nonagricultural sectors, and (3) the role of petroleum as a key sector in Mexican development.

Table 4. **Accounts in the final** *FAM*

Production sectors:	Institutions:
Foodgrain agriculture	*Campesinos* (small farmers)
Livestock	Agricultural workers
Other agriculture	Commercial farmers
Petroleum	Urban workers
Fertilizer	Urban capitalists
Agricultural processing	Merchants
Industry	Urban marginals
Services	
Commerce	Exogenous accounts:
	Government
	Capital
	Rest-of-the-world

The household institution accounts include three rural household groups. They are rural workers; agribusiness, or large commercial-farm households; and campesinos, or small farm households, ranging from infrasubsistence households (households having fewer than 4 hectares of land) to subsistence households (4 to 8 hectares), to seasonal farmers, who produce occasional surpluses (8 to 12 hectares), to surplus-producing small-farm households. Urban household groups include urban workers, urban capitalists, merchants, and urban marginals.

There are the usual three exogenous accounts in the FAM: government, investment and the rest of the world.

29

II.7. MODELLING EXPENDITURE ELASTICITIES

Production in the FAM model is described by a Leontief fixed coefficient technology. In the short run, given existing technology, our aggregated production sectors are not likely to alter their relative input mixes substantially in response to changes in demand. By contrast, households are able to respond quickly to changes in income by altering their expenditure patterns. The assumption of unitary expenditure elasticities is one limitation of the conventional Social Accounting Matrix.

In our policy experiments, expenditure elasticities are allowed to vary with income for each household group, permitting households to adjust their expenditure patterns in response to income changes. Flexibility on the expenditure side is incorporated into the FAM model by substituting a matrix of marginal expenditure propensities — the expenditure derivatives with respect to income — for the basic income and calorie FAM expenditure coefficient matrix. (The FAM coefficient matrix is the FAM income flows matrix normalized by dividing each internal element by its respective column total.)

The matrix of marginal expenditure propensities is constructed from estimates of expenditure elasticities by Heien, Jarvis and Perali (1988), using the method of moments proposed by Greene (1981, 1983) and data from the 1977 Income and Expenditure Survey conducted by the Mexican Ministry of Planning and Budget. The effect of a change in household income from the base (1980) income level, DY, on household expenditures on good i is given by $Dc_i = b_i DY$, where b_i is the marginal budget share of good i. This is in contrast to the conventional Social Accounting Matrix assumption that $Dc_i = s_i DY$, where s_i is the average budget share of good i in the base period.

III

FAM MULTIPLIER ANALYSIS

Multiplier analysis is useful for examining the impact of changes in Mexican government policies and world market conditions as their repercussions spread through the economy. FAM multipliers are the basis for the scenario analysis and counterfactual experiments discussed in Chapter IV. We begin by describing the construction of the FAM multiplier matrix, the role of the expenditure-derivatives matrix, and the concept of calorie multipliers. We then present the estimated FAM and FAM multiplier matrices.

III.1. FAM MULTIPLIERS

In the FAM as in Leontief multiplier analysis, a vector of exogenous flows (x) multiplied by a matrix multiplier (M) yields a consistent level of endogenous flows (y):

$$y = Mx$$

where $M = [I - A]_{-1}$ and A is an (n x n) coefficient matrix of endogenous FAM accounts.

The FAM coefficient matrix corresponding to Table 3 can be partitioned into four submatrices of endogenous accounts: a Leontief input-output matrix corresponding to the two production activities (denoted "L"), a value-added coefficient matrix describing payments to factor inputs ("F"), a matrix describing the distribution of value-added across households and other institutions ("D") and an expenditure coefficients matrix representing average budget shares ("E"). To calculate the multiplier, the expenditure submatrix is replaced by an expenditure-derivatives submatrix, which describes changes in average budget shares with respect to income. Letting "DE" denote a matrix of differences between marginal and average budget shares, the coefficient matrix of endogenous FAM accounts has the following form:

$$
A = \begin{bmatrix} L & 0 & E+\Delta E \\ F & 0 & 0 \\ 0 & D & 0 \end{bmatrix}
$$

31

Computing $[I-A]^{-1}$ by partitioning yields the FAM multiplier matrix:

$$M = (I-A)^{-1} \begin{bmatrix} M_1 & M_1(E+\Delta E)D & M_1(E+\Delta E) \\ FM_1 & I-F(E+\Delta E)D & FM_1(E+\Delta E) \\ DFM_1 & D[I-F(E+\Delta E)D] & I+DFM_1(E+\Delta E) \end{bmatrix}$$

where $M_1 = [I-A-(E+\Delta E)DF]^{-1}$. M_1 represents the production-multiplier effect of exogenous income changes as these swirl through the value added, distribution and expenditure accounts into the production account. The proliferation of the matrix ΔE in the FAM multiplier matrix suggests that adjustments in expenditure patterns in response to income changes potentially may play an important role in determining the impact of exogenous shocks on production, income and expenditures in the economy.

III.2. THE CALORIE MULTIPLIER

A novel feature of the FAM multiplier matrix is that it contains calorie multipliers as well as multipliers on income flows. The calorie multipliers capture the effect of exogenous income changes on calorie flows in the economy. Just as income multipliers can be decomposed into three effects (Pyatt and Round, 1979; Stone, 1985), the calorie multiplier has three components. To see this, consider an exogenous change in household income. The initial impact of the income change is to alter the flow of calories within the household accounts through the effect of the income change on household expenditures on calorie goods. This is the intragroup multiplier — the calorie-consumption effect of the initial income injection that remains within the original, recipient account D.

The change in household expenditure, in turn, affects other accounts in the FAM. For example, it affects the demand for goods that originate from the production account, thereby altering income flows and calorie production in the production submatrix. This is the intergroup multiplier.

Changes in income and calorie flows in other accounts, in turn, have a feedback effect on the original, income-recipient accounts. Changes in production in response to changes in household expenditures result in changes in the flows of value added back into the household accounts. The result is successive rounds of (progressively dampened) income and calorie feedbacks into the household accounts. This produces an "extragroup calorie multiplier" analogous to, and concurrent with, the extragroup income multiplier familiar to students of the conventional Social Accounting Matrix analysis.

III.3. THE ESTIMATED FOOD ACCOUNTING MATRIX

The complete FAM consists of 16 endogenous income accounts and 11 endogenous calorie accounts. In our estimation of the income and calorie multipliers, income and calorie accounts are woven together into a (27x27) matrix. For purposes of presentation the complete FAM is quite large and cumbersome; we shall therefore separate the income and calorie sides of the FAM in the discussion that follows. Interactions between the two sides of the FAM multiplier matrix will be highlighted further in the policy experiments described in Chapter IV.

The production core of the FAM was constructed by aggregating inputoutput tables provided by the National Institute of Economics, Geography and Information (INEIGI) of the Mexican government. The input-output tables also provided information on final demand totals, on labour and capital value-added by sector, and on the import content of production by sector.

Household budget shares and the distribution of value-added by household group were obtained from an analysis of the 1977 National Expenditure Survey by Heien, Jarvis and Perali (1988) and from Lustig (1982a). The distribution of value-added closely follows that of Lustig's 1975 Social Accounting Matrix, which was constructed using 1977 income distribution and expenditure data (Lustig, 1982b).

Data on macro balances from Mexican government and World Bank sources were used to fill in the remainder of the income side of the FAM: government revenues and expenditures, the foreign trade balance, foreign borrowing, and foreign and domestic savings. Rural-to-urban migrant remittances in the FAM were estimated on the basis of survey data (CENIET, 1978; Adelman, Taylor and Vogel, 1989). Capital flight (from urban and rich rural households) and foreign migrant remittances (primarily to rural households) were estimated as residuals, inasmuch as no reliable numbers are available for these flows.

A RAS procedure was used to achieve consistency between row and column totals in the household consumption submatrix (elements (1,10) through (9,16) of the FAM), but only at the margin, once near-consistency had been reached. A limited RAS was performed separately on the household savings vector, to ensure consistency between household savings and (unconsumed) household income.

III.3.1. FAM Income Accounts

The FAM income flows are summarized in Table 5. Once these flows are normalized on total expenditures in each sector, Table 5 becomes the A matrix in Section III.1, containing the Leontief Input-Output matrix in its northwest (9x9) quadrant.

On the agricultural side, one of the most striking features of the FAM income flows is the relatively weak backward linkages but relatively strong forward linkages between basic grains and the rest of the Mexican economy. The demand for domestically produced inputs by this sector equals just over 10 per cent of the value of total basic grains output, and in no case does the demand for inputs from non-basic-grain sectors exceed 2.2 per cent of the value of basic grain production. Forward linkages, by contrast, are relatively strong: 42 per cent of basic grain output is absorbed by intermediate demand. The strongest intermediate demand for basic grain output is by food processing; it consists primarily of the demand for maize by tortilla processors. Forty-six per cent of basic grain output is absorbed directly by consumption demand. However, nearly 33 per cent of the apparent demand for basic foodgrains in 1980 was satisfied not by domestic producers but by imports.

The importance of basic grains as a staple crop on poor peasant farms is reflected by the low intensity of modern input use by basic grains relative to other agriculture. Fertilizer demand represents less than one per cent of the value of basic grain output, compared with over 3 per cent of the value of other agricultural production. The demand for other industrial inputs relative to output is more than 3.5 times greater for "other agriculture" than for basic grains.

Table 5. 1980 Mexico *FAM* income flows

	Basic grains (1)	Livestock (2)	Other agriculture (3)	Petroleum (4)	Fertilizer (5)	Agricultural processing (6)	Industry (7)	Services (8)	Commerce (9)	Campesinos (10)
1. Basic grains	4 695	7 715			10	26 519	1 450	840		13 305
2. Livestock		502	72		32	146 908	25 708	896		3 531
3. Other agriculture		28 677	3 409	39 279	90	40 624	40 334	23 776		6 771
4. Petroleum	406	786	3 246		147	2 677	396	23 776	2 087	290
5. Fertilizer	812		6 489					84		
6. Agricultural processing	1 966	28 946	386	1	8	81 443	12 515	3 643	53 598	35 921
7. Industry	560	11 104	15 713	5 560	4 328	38 891	713 913	123 848	126 912	28 386
8. Services	888	4 527	4 479	8 546	418	28 758	136 819	218 412	12 014	28 326
9. Commerce		5 811	7 094	4 058	338	46 533	155 372	37 956		33 160
10. Campesinos	59 473	31 765	44 167							
11. Agricultural workers	18 109	31 657	44 017							
12. Agricultural business	6 609	56 672	78 799							
13. Urban workers				17 529	1 656	67 092	504 510	567 931	176 513	
14. Urban capitalists				81 576		144 232	491 275	732 483	595 721	
15. Merchant capitalists						17 036	62 998	90 552	68 705	
16. Urban marginals	−1 260	541	2 500		856	14 769	60 854	13 888	256 378	
17. Government										7 800
18. Savings	398	614	3 180	6 312	926	51 253	179 852	32 033	2 212	3 702
19. Imports										
20. Total	92 656	209 317	208 551	162 861	8 809	706 735	2 385 996	1 846 342	1 294 140	161 192

	Agricultural workers (11)	Agricultural business (12)	Urban workers (13)	Urban capital (14)	Merchants (15)	Urban marginals (16)	Government (17)	Investment (18)	Exports (19)	Total (20)
1. Basic grains	6 122	927	7 264	4 654	2 266	7 840		10 100	1 239	92 656
2. Livestock	2 131	1 905	16 379	10 215	5 055	4 693	88	12 957	2 591	209 317
3. Other agriculture	4 089	3 654	31 412	19 591	9 695	9 000	651	14 817	9 525	208 551
4. Petroleum	186	751	2 685	2 507	985	244	1 620	2 301	38 611	162 861
5. Fertilizer							156	45	680	8 809
6. Agricultural processing	26 915	20 876	202 635	123 225	63 034	54 892	657	25 843	25 795	706 735
7. Industry	18 038	20 004	212 139	130 625	56 262	33 351	18 484	809 379	90 407	2 385 996
8. Services	31 014	39 956	384 806	293 854	125 957	51 049	281 644	22 862	57 443	1 846 342
9. Commerce	26 358	26 959	262 663	180 851	81 403	48 141	4 930	152 741	206 870	1 294 140
10. Campesinos			9 180			3 713			12 894	161 192

34

#	Account	11	12	13	14	15	16	17	18	19	Total
12.	Agricultural business							168 862			142 080
13.	Urban workers							23 514	−27 571		1 476 522
14.	Urban capitalists							10 815	−97 178		1 294 326
15.	Merchant capitalists							10 109	−30 852		575 684
16.	Urban marginals							623			249 400
17.	Government		10 015	103 782	96 418	41 986	27 878	150 732	225 821		677 926
18.	Savings		13 650	197 044	406 722	177 934	5 203	5 041	528 066		1 207 581
19.	Imports	2 512	3 383	38 138	25 664	11 107		156 536			528 066
20.	Total	117 365	142 080	1 476 522	1 294 326	575 684	249 400	677 926	1 207 581	528 066	13 345 549

Source: See text for details on construction of the FAM.

35

The livestock demand for feedgrains is reflected in this sector's large purchases from the basic grains sector (cell 1,2), from other agriculture (3,2) and from the agricultural processing sector (6,2), through which most imported and domestically-produced sorghum for livestock production is channeled. Fourteen per cent of total sector-3 output is absorbed directly by the livestock sector; an additional amount is absorbed indirectly through agricultural processing. Inputs from the basic grains, other agriculture and agricultural processing sectors represent 31 per cent of the total value of livestock production. They reflect very strong backward linkages from the livestock sector. Most livestock output is absorbed by the food processing sector and by domestic consumption demand (91 per cent); only 1 per cent of livestock output was exported in 1980.

The intersectoral linkages in Table 5 are further illustrated in the FAM income multiplier matrix (Table 6), which corresponds to the M matrix in Section III.2. The basic grains account in the income multiplier matrix reflects the strong forward linkages between this and other sectors of the economy (Row 1). Despite weak backward linkages between basic grains and other production sectors in the FAM, Table 6 shows strong backward SAM linkages from this sector (Column 1). The SAM linkages are due mostly to the large positive effect of increased demand for basic grains on household incomes — especially campesino incomes — which in turn generate new consumer demand for domestically-produced goods. The livestock demand for feedgrains is also evident in Table 6 (Column 2): a one-dollar increase in exogenous demand for livestock products generates a $1.02 increase in this sector's demand for intermediate inputs from the other three food-related sectors. Part of the explanation for this large feedgrain multiplier comes from the consumption side of the FAM: an increase in exogenous demand for livestock products results in a significant increase in household incomes, which in turn generates further increases in consumer demand in the economy.

Table 6 also provides useful information about household income linkages in the Mexican economy. The strongest income linkages for campesino households, not surprisingly, are with the basic grains sector: a one-dollar increase in exogenous demand for basic grains produces a $1.02 increase in the flow of value-added into campesino households. Income linkages between campesino households and the other two agricultural sectors are only one-third as large as this basic grain linkage. Increased demand for basic foodgrains has a relatively weak effect on rural worker incomes, however. This reflects the comparatively small contribution of hired-labour value added to foodgrain production on small peasant farms, and it suggests that the familiar policy tradeoff between increasing small-farmer incomes and increasing agriculturalworker incomes is particularly relevant to Mexico. The income multiplier matrix also reflects strong rural-urban income linkages, indicated by a large positive effect of increased demand for agricultural commodities on urban incomes. This effect operates through the strong positive effect that an increase in rural incomes has on the demand for urban-produced goods, and it suggests the relevance of rural income-led industrialization policies in the Mexican context.

III.3.2. FAM Calorie Accounts

FAM calorie flows are summarized in Table 7. The entries in the Table are all in per capita terms; they were obtained by dividing gross calorie flows by the 1980 Mexican population. Gross calorie flows were calculated by multiplying total production volumes of various calorie supplying commodities by the usable portion of the commodity times the

36

Table 6. **1980 Mexico _FAM_ income multiplier matrix**

	Basic grains (1)	Livestock (2)	Other agriculture (3)	Petroleum (4)	Fertilizer (5)	Agricultural processing (6)	Industry (7)	Services (8)
1. Basic grains	1.1841	0.1263	0.0780	0.0116	0.0308	0.1058	0.0346	0.0386
2. Livestock	0.1715	1.1755	0.1414	0.0311	0.0784	0.3474	0.0915	0.1023
3. Other agriculture	0.1480	0.2736	1.1380	0.0270	0.0773	0.1918	0.0918	0.0876
4. Petroleum	0.0587	0.0595	0.0725	1.3322	0.0599	0.0500	0.0665	0.0585
5. Fertilizer	0.0154	0.0100	0.0369	0.0010	1.0199	0.0072	0.0036	0.0033
6. Agricultural processing	0.5593	0.6203	0.4654	0.1034	0.2609	1.5117	0.3039	0.3388
7. Industry	0.8743	0.8315	0.8585	0.2482	1.1607	0.6911	1.9404	0.6756
8. Services	0.9493	0.9348	0.9442	0.3153	0.6791	0.7947	0.7623	1.8966
9. Commerce	0.6954	0.6478	0.6486	0.1833	0.4469	0.5605	0.5105	0.5018
10. Campesinos	1.0191	0.3878	0.3360	0.0235	0.0620	0.1971	0.0711	0.0764
11. Rural workers	0.1550	0.2348	0.2710	0.0133	0.0351	0.1020	0.0408	0.0425
12. Agricultural business	0.1298	0.3964	0.4669	0.0182	0.0493	0.1609	0.0582	0.0593
13. Urban workers	0.6340	0.6189	0.6193	0.3278	0.7382	0.6173	0.7511	0.8338
14. Urban capitalists	0.6708	0.6687	0.6463	0.1973	0.5616	0.7661	0.7640	0.9607
15. Merchant capitalists	0.3201	0.2982	0.2986	0.0844	0.2057	0.2580	0.2350	0.2310
16. Urban marginals	0.1200	0.1171	0.1146	0.0342	0.0940	0.1234	0.1230	0.1457

	Commerce (9)	Campesinos (10)	Agricultural workers (11)	Agricultural business (12)	Urban workers (13)	Urban capitalists (14)	Merchant capitalists (15)	Urban marginals (16)
1. Basic grains	0.0317	0.1402	0.1102	0.0473	0.0445	0.0323	0.0339	0.0843
2. Livestock	0.0834	0.1760	0.1749	0.1297	0.1208	0.0893	0.0946	0.1638
3. Other agriculture	0.0709	0.1520	0.1465	0.1106	0.1024	0.0754	0.0793	0.1381
4. Petroleum	0.0349	0.0519	0.0538	0.0498	0.0433	0.0339	0.0338	0.0469
5. Fertilizer	0.0027	0.0063	0.0058	0.0041	0.0038	0.0028	0.0029	0.0053
6. Agricultural processing	0.2770	0.5721	0.5861	0.4249	0.4028	0.2958	0.3145	0.5418
7. Industry	0.5201	0.8506	0.8456	0.7037	0.6844	0.5095	0.5108	0.7495
8. Services	0.7197	0.9338	1.0672	0.9403	0.8895	0.7088	0.7059	0.9163
9. Commerce	1.3956	0.6912	0.7270	0.5913	0.5625	0.4307	0.4370	0.6429
10. Campesinos	0.0617	1.1837	0.1587	0.0911	0.0915	0.0626	0.0658	0.1485
11. Rural workers	0.0340	0.0728	1.0694	0.0497	0.0521	0.0343	0.0360	0.0773
12. Agricultural business	0.0482	0.1045	0.1014	1.0750	0.0696	0.0514	0.0542	0.0948
13. Urban workers	0.5523	0.6224	0.6687	0.5652	1.5387	0.4168	0.4188	0.5855
14. Urban capitalists	0.4491	0.6623	0.7171	0.6047	0.5760	1.4465	0.4494	0.6284
15. Merchant capitalists	0.6424	0.3182	0.3346	0.2722	0.2589	0.1982	1.2012	0.2959
16. Urban marginals	0.1298	0.1187	0.1274	0.1063	0.1013	0.0782	0.0789	1.1119

calorie content per usable unit. Data on calorie content and usable shares of food commodities were provided by the Mexican National Nutrition Institute.

Table 7 shows that Mexico's largest gross production of calories comes from the food-processing sector (2273 calories per capita per year). This number is somewhat misleading, however, because food processing is actually an inefficient net producer of calories, as illustrated by this sector's large intermediate demand for calories from other sectors and from imports. Similarly, although livestock generates 932 calories annually per capita, livestock calorie value-added is actually negative: more calories of feedgrains go into the production of meat than come out. The basic grains sector is characterized by few backward calorie linkages and strong forward calorie linkages; it has far and away the highest per capita calorie value added of the four food sectors.

The calorie flows matrix has two rows that are not analogous to the transactions matrix: the wastage row and the net calorie transfers row. The wastage row represents the calorie losses in processing and in storage, which occur both in the producing sectors and in the households themselves. About 9 per cent of the calories produced are wasted. The "net calorie gain" row indicates the transfer of calorie value added among households. The agricultural households produce more calories than they consume and the urban households consume more calories than they produce. This row therefore has positive entries for rural households and negative entries for urban households. The sum of net calorie transfers across all accounts must add up to zero. There is also a positive entry in the net transfer row for exports. This entry indicates that there has been a net calorie gain through international trade.

The calorie flows are expressed in average daily kilo calories per capita. To see the actual number of kilo calories consumed by the average Mexican person in 1980, one must take the total number of calories consumed by each household institution, subtract from it the wastage and net calorie gains, and add up the result across all household institutions. This works out to about 2850 calories per capita, a number that is consistent with the results of the only national nutrition study for 1975, extrapolated to 1980 by using the marginal propensities to consume calories. The composition of calories by food source also matches the 1975 study very closely.

To derive the daily calorie consumption of an average person in each household group requires dividing the total calories consumed by the particular household institution by the share of population in that institution. Based on estimates of the number of persons in each household institution, this procedure yields the following average daily calorie consumption for an average person in each household institution: campesinos, 2381; agricultural workers, 2201; commercial farmers, 3389; marginal urban workers, 2168; urban workers, 3224; capitalists, 4305; and merchants, 3839. Since there is a distribution of calorie consumption around the average in each household group, groups whose average calorie consumption is close to the minimum FAO standard for an active life clearly have a substantial proportion of persons with a calorie intake that is below the minimum. The calorie FAM suggests that the groups with a large proportion of persons at risk of malnutrition are agricultural workers, urban marginals, and campesinos. This is consistent with studies of nutritional status by the Mexican National Nutrition Institute.

The calorie FAM also provides information on the composition of calorie intake by different household categories. Campesinos derive about 53 per cent of their calories from grains and only 3 per cent of their calories from livestock. Agricultural workers derive about 47 per cent of their calories from basic grains and 3.4 per cent from livestock. Commercial farmers derive the bulk of their calories from processed food (52 per cent), 9 per cent of their

Table 7. 1980 Mexico *FAM* calorie flows

	Grain calories (1)	Livestock calories (2)	Other agricultural calories (3)	Agricultural processing calories (4)	Campesinos (5)	Agricultural workers (6)	Agricultural business (7)	Urban workers (8)	Urban capitalists (9)	Merchant capitalists (10)	Urban marginals (11)	Investment (12)	Wastage (13)	Export calories (14)	Total (15)
1. Grain calories	100.99	165.95	—	570.42	300.84	138.20	20.88	163.99	105.06	51.15	176.30	217.25		56.10	2 067.13
2. Livestock calories		2.20	0.32	644.93	16.68	10.07	8.99	77.37	48.25	23.88	22.17	56.88		20.28	932.02
3. Other agricultural calories		616.84	5.42	64.59	11.29	6.81	6.09	52.36	32.65	16.16	15.00	14.97	−571.24	18.93	289.87
4. Agricultural processing calories		622.63	1.00	211.75	90.37	67.60	52.65	508.37	309.38	157.96	137.82	67.19	−14.18	32.33	2 273.23
5. Campesinos	1 388.90	−125.79	74.89										328.39		1 666.39
6. Agricultural workers	422.91	−125.36	74.54										311.72		683.81
7. Agricultural business	154.34	−224.42	133.71										533.81		597.44
8. Urban workers													51.00		51.00
9. Urban capitalists													31.52		31.52
10. Merchant capitalists													15.86		15.86
11. Urban marginals													23.25		23.25
12. Savings					27.52		9.85	117.58	171.21	84.69	45.22				456.07
13. Wastage				561.55	32.52	16.85	5.94	51.00	31.52	15.86	23.25				738.49
14. Import calories				220.00	117.00	54.00	8.00	28.00	18.00	9.00	30.00				484.00
15. Net calorie transfers					1 070.17	390.28	485.04	−947.67	−684.55	−342.84	−426.51	99.78		356.36	0.06
16. Total	2 067.14	932.05	289.88	2 273.24	1 666.39	683.81	597.44	51.00	31.52	15.86	23.25	456.07	738.49	484.00	10 310.14

39

calories from livestock, and only 20 per cent of their calories from basic grain. Urban workers consume most of their calories in processed form (58 per cent) and 9 per cent from livestock directly (about a third of the processed-food category for urban groups consists of meat). Almost 60 per cent of the calories consumed by capitalists and merchants come from processed foods and only about 20 per cent from basic grains. By contrast, urban marginals derive about 40 per cent of their calories from basic grains and only 17 per cent from processed foods.

Another interesting piece of information that can be derived from the calorie-flow FAM is the price of calories for each calorie-producing sector and for each household institution. We can calculate the implicit calorie prices by dividing the peso totals by the corresponding calorie totals. The cost of providing a calorie of basic grains to the entire population for one year is 44.8 million pesos; this cost for a livestock calorie is 224.6 million (about five times as much as a grain calorie). For "other agriculture," consisting mostly of fruits and vegetables, the cost is 721.6 million; and for processed foods the cost is 310 million pesos.

Two types of calorie multipliers can be constructed on the basis of Tables 6 and 7. A FAM calorie-income multiplier matrix is used in our policy experiments to explore the effects of exogenous income changes on calorie flows. It is an (11 by 11) matrix constructed on the four calorie-producing and calorie-purchasing production sectors (basic grains, livestock, other agriculture and food processing) and the seven household sectors. On the production side, element (i,j) in the calorie multiplier submatrix is calculated as the corresponding income multiplier divided by the average price of calories for sector i. Average calorie prices for sector i are estimated using information on calorie contents of various food commodities provided by the Mexican National Nutrition Institute, food commodity prices, and sector i's food commodity input shares. On the expenditure side, element (i,n) of the calorie multiplier matrix is estimated as the corresponding income multiplier divided by the marginal price of calories for household group n. Marginal calorie prices are obtained in a manner analogous to average calorie prices on the production side but using marginal, rather than average, household propensities to consume calorie-supplying commodities. That is, calorie contents of the calorie-providing commodities, prices of these commodities, and the marginal shares of these commodities in household budgets are used to estimate the marginal price of calories for our household groups. The rationale behind using marginal, rather than average, calorie prices on the household side is that, because household budget allocations across food and nonfood commodities change as household incomes increase, a given change in household income will not have the same effect on calorie intake at all income levels.

A second type of calorie-multiplier matrix measures the impact of exogenous changes in calorie final demand to calorie flows in the system. This "physical calorie multiplier" matrix appears in Table 8. It highlights major linkages in the Mexican calorie economy. The inefficiency of livestock at converting feedgrain calories to meat calories is illustrated in Column 2 by significant backward calorie linkages from this sector to the feedgrain-producing sectors. Large backward calorie linkages are also evident in other agriculture and in agricultural processing, although they are much smaller than those of the livestock sector. The strong induced demand for calories by these sectors is partly indirect: an increase in final demand for calories from a given sector ultimately leads to changes in calorie demand by households that receive value-added from that sector. Large backward calorie linkages from sectors 2, 3 and 4 reflect in part the relatively inefficient calorie-consumption patterns of households that participate in these sectors. Smaller linkages are visible for basic grains, produced primarily in campesino households in which demand elasticities for calorie-inefficient foods are comparatively small.

40

Table 8. **1980 Mexico *FAM* calorie multiplier matrix**

		Grain calories	Livestock calories	Other agricultural calories	Agricultural processing calories	Campesinos	Agricultural workers
		(1)	(2)	(3)	(4)	(5)	(6)
1.	Grain calories	2.7813	1.6331	1.6185	1.3312	1.7629	1.7096
2.	Livestock calories	0.3615	1.5324	0.4433	0.5933	0.3392	0.3697
3.	Other agricultural calories	0.3400	1.1303	1.4349	0.4926	0.3198	0.3456
4.	Agricultural processing calories	0.9133	1.6020	1.1224	1.8918	0.8530	0.9467
5.	Campesinos	1.9078	1.1825	1.3983	0.9416	2.2213	1.1881
6.	Agricultural workers	0.6078	0.4187	0.6405	0.3192	0.3973	1.3889
7.	Agricultural business	0.2774	0.2743	0.6760	0.1838	0.1974	0.1980
8.	Urban workers						
9.	Urban capitalists						
10.	Merchant capitalists						
11.	Urban marginals						

		Agricultural business	Urban workers	Urban capitalists	Merchant capitalists	Urban marginals
		(7)	(8)	(9)	(10)	(11)
1.	Grain calories	1.4890	1.5253	1.5338	1.5244	1.8151
2.	Livestock calories	0.5389	0.5705	0.5689	0.5692	0.4601
3.	Other agricultural calories	0.5064	0.5320	0.5314	0.5306	0.4311
4.	Agricultural processing calories	1.3643	1.4689	1.4594	1.4669	1.1719
5.	Campesinos	1.0586	1.0853	1.0910	1.0845	1.2689
6.	Agricultural workers	0.3624	0.3721	0.3739	0.3717	0.4203
7.	Agricultural business	1.2150	0.2219	0.2226	0.2215	0.2236
8.	Urban workers		1.0			
9.	Urban capitalists			1.0		
10.	Merchant capitalists				1.0	
11.	Urban marginals					1.0

IV

SCENARIO ANALYSES AND COUNTERFACTUAL EXPERIMENTS

Trends in world markets, Mexican development policy and changes in patterns of consumer demand serve as inputs into food and agricultural trade scenario analyses and counterfactual studies. The FAM developed in chapter III is the foundation for projecting impacts of future world agricultural and oil market scenarios and Mexican policies on the Mexican food economy and on agricultural trade. Alternative policy and worldmarket scenarios which are considered are:

1. High versus low world food price scenarios

2. High versus low world oil price scenarios

3. Mexican development policy scenarios:
   a. Continuation of the present dualistic agricultural development policy;
   b. Movement to a unimodal agricultural development model that emphasizes increases in production on small farms;
   c. A "populist" development model, combining food subsidies with high wages; and
   d. An "austerity" model, combining wage-repression with the elimination of food subsidies.

The scenarios above imply 16 world-market cum domestic-policy combinations. We did not examine all such combinations, since some domestic policies are inherently unlikely under particular world-price scenarios. Specifically, the adoption of the unimodal and populist strategies is likely only when world prices for petroleum are high. By the same token, the adoption of the austerity program of wage repression is likely only when international prices for petroleum are low. The results of our experiments, however, suggest that the choice of these policies may, in some cases, be ill-advised.

These experiments focus on what might be considered an equilibrium growth path under alternative policy and world-market scenarios in the medium run. Their intent, therefore, is not to replicate what actually happened under Mexico's structural adjustment policies of the 1980s[4]. The catastrophic performance of the Mexican economy from 1980 to 1986 reflects extreme policy responses to debt crisis and to unusually large falls in world oil prices. This period, therefore, would not provide a useful basis for exploring the implications of alternative growth strategies in the longer run. Our "base" strategy, therefore, reproduces the growth trajectory between 1974 and 1984.

To achieve comparability among strategies, we first extrapolated the existing development strategy ten years and then designed variants on the base strategy, keeping the base trend constant except as indicated by the particular strategy variant. Each strategy variant was then "exposed" to different world market conditions for oil and basic grains.

The results of the experiments are reproduced in Tables 9 through 14. We first turn to a specific discussion of each of our strategies. We then discuss how the strategies are affected by different world market trends. While the results are discussed in quantitative terms, their interpretation is intended to be qualitative. That is, the results should be taken as indicative of trends and orders of magnitude, rather than literally.

IV.1. THE BIMODAL AGRICULTURAL STRATEGY

This strategy, which is a continuation of the present Mexican development pattern, was designed by extrapolating the changes in production sector by sector and trends in world prices between 1974 and 1984, and then letting these changes percolate through the system. The multiplier matrix of Table 6 was used together with a calorietransformation matrix to calculate the primary and second-round repercussions of the extrapolated changes in production. The calorie transformation matrix has zeros everywhere except in positions ij , where i is the index of a calorie-producing output or income flow and j is the index of the calorie flow. The non-zero entries are one over the marginal price of calories. For the producing sectors, the marginal and average prices of calories are the same; for the household income flows, the marginal calorie prices were obtained from the changes in the composition of consumption indicated by our marginal propensities to consume. The "base" bimodal strategy assumes a continuation of the agricultural bimodal strategy, production subsidies on inputs to commercial farmers, and price subsidies to urban consumers of grain. It also assumes a continuation of import-substitution industrialization and the continuation of international price trends during 1974-84: falling grain prices and rising oil prices. (A logarithmic time trend fitted to oil prices indicates a mildly rising trend of 1.3 per cent per year for the period.)

The results of the continuation of the bimodal cum import-substitution strategy are quite favourable in growth terms: a 66 percent increase in GDP over the ten-year period, implying an average rate of growth of income of 5 per cent per year and a tripling of oil production. There is also a continuation of the usual patterns of structural change that accompany the late stages of economic development: a reduction in the share of agriculture in total value added (by 11 per cent) and an increase in the share of services (by 5 per cent). But population growth at the 1980-86 rate of 2.55 per cent per year eats up much of the benefits of overall output and income growth on per capita incomes (Table 13). Per-capita incomes of campesinos, agricultural workers and commercial farmers rise between 32 and 38 per cent over the tenyear period; those of urban groups rise by between 9 and 26 per cent in ten years. Rapid population growth, fed by migration, substantially depresses urban per-capita income growth.

The consequences of the bimodal strategy for the trade and government budget balances are favourable. As we shall see below, however, the trade balance and the government deficit are quite sensitive to world-price scenarios. There is a fall in the government deficit from the high 5.3 per cent of GDP in 1980 to a still high but more manageable 3.6 per cent of GDP, implying a slackening of inflationary pressures. To calculate the government budget deficit,

43

Table 9. Sectoral performance under alternative development strategies and price scenarios

	Strategies													
Sectors	Bimodal				Unimodal			Populist			Wage repression		
	Base	HH[1]	LH[1]	LL[1]	Base	HH[1]	HL[1]	Base	HH[1]	HL[1]	Base	LH[1]	HL[1]
	% of 1980				% of bimodal base scenario								
Basic grains	165.6	104.5	102.9	94.4	179.3	188.4	161.8	102.1	107.5	100.8	73.7	78.2	72.5
Livestock	147.2	100.5	93.4	93.6	102.6	102.6	93.7	102.6	103.9	101.2	62.8	62.7	62.6
Other agriculture	138.7	100.2	97.0	94.5	104.0	104.5	95.9	100.9	101.7	100.2	66.9	67.1	67.1
Petroleum	276.3	146.9	73.1	72.2	101.3	148.0	145.1	97.0	143.7	144.8	61.7	46.0	46.0
Fertilizer	195.4	97.2	102.3	99.6	108.5	106.4	99.3	97.7	96.2	94.7	79.9	83.1	85.5
Agricultural processing	152.9	100.1	96.4	93.7	100.7	101.4	92.2	104.0	105.3	102.7	70.8	71.1	71.3
Industry	155.7	99.6	99.1	97.2	102.5	102.1	97.6	98.3	98.9	97.6	89.4	89.9	90.0
Services	184.6	100.2	92.1	89.8	103.1	102.9	90.5	88.8	89.9	88.3	75.2	75.9	76.1
Commerce	149.7	98.9	98.8	96.8	103.8	102.9	96.2	103.5	111.6	101.5	76.5	78.5	78.6

1. The scenarios represent international oil and grain price regimes. The first letter characterizes the oil price regime (H = high or L = low) and the second food prices.

44

Table 10. **Macroeconomic performance under alternative development strategies and price scenarios**

Figure in billions of 1980 pesos unless otherwise indicated

Performance criterion	Strategies													
	Bimodal					Unimodal			Populist			Wage repression		
	Base	HH[1]	HL[1]	LH[1]	LL[1]	Base	HH[1]	HL[1]	Base	HH[1]	HL[1]	Base	LH[1]	HL[1]
GDP	7082	7104	6999	6810	6631	7405	7429	6770	6718	6818	6672	3201	3161	3140
GDP ratio to 1980	1.66	1.66	1.63	1.59	1.55	1.73	1.74	1.58	1.57	1.59	1.56	0.75	0.74	0.735
Government deficit														
Changes from 1980														
Receipts	494	596	574	407	385	525	628	605	477	596	575	224	201	198
Expenditures	524	548	500	548	500	569	593	545	605	622	588	443	460	426
New deficit	−256	−178	−152	−367	−341	−270	−191	−286	−334	−232	−237	−445	−485	−454
Deficit % of GDP	−3.61	−2.5	−2.2	−5.4	−5.1	−3.6	−2.6	−4.2	−5.3	−3.7	−3.5	−13.9	−15.3	−14.5
Trade														
Changes from 1980														
Total agric. imports	44	39	40	35	45	−100	−88	−59	42	34	43	−5	−11	−4
Grain	23	15	30	16	28	−122	−111	−76	22	15	23	−4	−10	−3
Livestock	8	8	6	7	6	8	8	6	8	8	8	1	1	1
Other agriculture	13	16	4	12	11	14	15	11	12	13	12	−2	−2	−2
Non-food imports	283	306	241	277	238	326	336	316	275	305	266	243	243	239
Total imports	327	345	281	312	283	226	248	257	317	339	309	238	232	235
Total exports	256	349	348	238	237	260	360	357	221	308	306	407	406	406
Trade balance														
New trade balance	−233	−156	−219	−226	−198	−118	−40	−52	−248	−183	−155	+17	+22	+19
% of exports	−35.2	−21.5	−31.1	−36.8	−32.3	−18.5	−5.4	−7.1	−41.5	−26.7	−22.7	+2.2	+2.8	+2.4

1. The scenarios represent international oil and grain price regimes. The first letter characterizes the oil price regime (H=high or L=low) and the second food prices.

45

Table 11. Growth in class income under alternative development strategies and price scenarios

	Strategies															
	Bimodal					Unimodal			Populist			Wage repression		
Household groups	% of base					% of bimodal base scenario								
	Base	HH[1]	HL[1]	LH[1]	LL[1]	Base	HH[1]	HL[1]	Base	HH[1]	HL[1]	Base	LH[1]	HL[1]
Rural														
Campesinos	149.4	100.5	90.7	101.0	96.1	146.5	151.3	132.5	102.3	103.6	101.4	64.9	64.7	67.1
Agricultural workers	144.0	99.0	90.4	100.1	96.6	101.2	102.2	93.8	102.3	102.2	101.5	71.8	73.1	74.1
Large farmers	143.3	100.5	92.0	97.1	94.1	102.2	102.7	94.3	101.7	103.1	100.8	73.9	73.6	73.9
Urban														
Marginals	164.1	100.9	90.5	96.6	92.8	104.1	103.8	92.9	108.0	110.4	105.7	47.5	47.3	45.9
Workers	167.9	100.9	93.1	95.7	93.5	102.7	103.5	95.2	107.7	109.8	107.7	46.9	47.0	46.5
Capitalists	175.9	100.1	90.4	94.7	92.3	102.8	102.8	92.8	83.2	83.8	82.6	28.7	28.1	27.6
Merchants	152.3	99.1	92.4	98.9	96.6	104.1	103.1	95.7	99.3	100.5	97.3	54.2	52.1	51.7

1. The scenarios represent international oil and grain price regimes. The first letter characterizes the oil price regime (H = high or L = low) and the second food prices.

Table 12. Functional distribution of income under alternative development strategies and price scenarios
Income shares, %

	Strategies														
	Bimodal					Unimodal			Populist			Wage repression		
Household groups	Base	HH[1]	HL[1]	LH[1]	LL[1]	Base	HH[1]	HL[1]	Base	HH[1]	HL[1]	Base	LH[1]	HL[1]
Rural														
Campesinos	3.6	3.6	4.0	4.1	4.2	5.1	5.2	5.0	4.5	3.8	3.8	5.4	5.4	5.6
Agricultural workers	2.5	2.5	2.9	3.0	3.0	2.5	2.5	2.5	3.2	2.6	2.6	4.2	4.3	4.4
Large farmers	3.1	3.1	3.5	3.6	3.6	3.0	3.0	3.0	3.8	3.2	3.2	5.2	5.2	5.2
Urban														
Marginals	6.2	6.2	6.1	6.1	6.3	6.1	6.1	6.0	8.1	6.9	6.7	6.7	6.7	6.5
Workers	37.2	37.5	37.3	36.7	36.5	36.6	36.8	37.1	29.5	41.3	41.4	39.9	40.4	40.5
Capitalists	34.2	34.1	31.8	31.7	31.6	33.6	33.5	33.2	34.8	28.9	29.1	22.4	22.2	21.9
Merchants	13.2	13.0	14.4	14.8	14.7	13.1	12.9	13.2	16.0	13.4	13.2	16.3	15.8	15.8

1. The scenarios represent international oil and grain price regimes. The first letter characterises the oil price regime (H = high or L = low) and the second food prices.

Table 13. **Growth in per capita[1] household income under alternative development strategies and price scenarios**

Percentage of 1980

Household groups	Bimodal					Unimodal			Populist			Wage repression		
	Base[1]	HH[2]	HL[2]	LH[2]	LL[1]	Base	HH[2]	HL[2]	Base	HH[2]	HL[2]	Base	LH[2]	HL[2]
Rural														
Campesinos	137.8	138.6	125.1	139.2	132.4	202.1	208.6	182.8	141.0	142.9	139.8	89.5	89.2	80.9
Agricultural workers	132.9	131.6	120.3	133.0	128.3	134.6	135.8	124.8	136.0	135.8	135.0	95.4	97.1	89.3
Large farmers	132.3	132.9	121.7	128.5	124.5	135.2	135.8	124.7	134.6	136.4	133.4	97.7	97.4	89.0
Urban														
Marginals	117.4	118.7	106.3	113.4	109.0	122.1	121.8	109.1	126.7	129.5	124.0	55.7	55.5	46.4
Workers	120.0	121.1	111.7	114.8	112.2	123.2	124.2	114.3	129.2	131.7	129.2	56.4	56.4	47.0
Capitalists	125.7	125.8	225.8	113.8	119.0	116.1	129.2	116.7	104.7	105.5	103.9	36.3	35.5	28.1
Merchants	109.0	108.0	100.8	107.8	105.3	113.4	112.3	104.4	108.3	109.5	106.1	59.0	56.7	52.2

1. Assuming continued national population growth at the 1980-86 level of 2.55 per cent and population growth net of migration to be 0.8 per cent for rural areas and 3.6 per cent for urban areas.
2. Based on preliminary population figures.

Table 14. Growth of per capita[1] calorie consumption under alternative development strategies and price scenarios

| | Base (1980) Daily calorie consumption per capita[2] | Strategies — % of bimodal base scenario | | | | | | | | | | | | | | | |
| | | % of 1980 | Bimodal | | | | Unimodal | | | Populist | | | Wage repression | | |
Household groups		Base	HH[3]	HL[3]	LH[3]	LL[3]	Base	HH[3]	HL[3]	Base	HH[3]	HL[3]	Base	LH[3]	HL[3]
Rural															
Campesinos	2 831	128.0	100.2	95.6	100.4	98.1	122.0	124.2	122.6	107.4	101.7	100.7	83.5	83.3	
Agricultural workers	2 201	125.3	99.6	96.1	100.0	98.6	100.5	100.9	97.5	101.0	100.9	100.6	88.5	89.0	89.4
Large farmers	3 389	122.7	100.1	98.3	100.8	98.8	100.5	100.6	98.8	100.4	100.7	100.2	94.5	94.4	94.5
Urban															
Marginals	2 168	106.1	100.3	96.7	98.8	97.5	101.4	101.3	97.6	102.7	103.6	101.9	82.0	81.9	81.5
Workers	3 224	104.2	100.2	98.6	99.2	98.7	100.5	100.7	99.1	101.5	101.9	101.5	89.7	89.7	89.6
Capitalists	4 305	103.9	100.0	98.6	99.2	98.9	100.4	100.4	99.0	97.6	97.5	97.5	89.7	89.6	89.6
Merchants	3 839	102.1	99.9	98.9	99.8	99.5	100.6	100.4	100.4	99.9	100.1	99.6	92.9	92.7	92.7

1. Assuming continued national population growth at the 1980-86 level of 2.55 per cent and population growth net of migration to be 0.8 per cent for rural areas and 3.6 per cent for urban areas.
2. Based on preliminary population figures.
3. The scenarios represent international oil and grain price regimes. The first letter characterizes the oil price regime (H = high or L = low) and the second food prices.

48

we extrapolated the changes in government receipts and government expenditures separately. We derived the changes in government receipts by multiplying the exogenous row of government-receipt shares in the FAM by the calculated changes in outputs and incomes. We computed the changes in government expenditures by adding to the exogenous column in the final demand matrix of the FAM the government expenditure shares on the exogenous flows (investment and capital), calculated as a ratio to the endogenous government expenditures.

The commodity trade balance rises at a somewhat slower rate than GDP, and the commodity trade deficit falls only slightly (from 3.5 to 3.1 per cent of GDP and from 40 per cent to 35 per cent of exports), despite aprojected large increase in oil exports from the 1974-84 base trend. The changes in the trade balance were calculated as follows: The changes in commodity-exports were projected from the exogenous vector in the FAM. The changes in agricultural imports were calculated by applying the shares of agricultural imports to outputs and incomes derived from an import-output matrix for 1980. Imports of basic grains are mostly for urban consumption, both directly and through food processing. Imports of livestock and dairy products are almost exclusively for inputs into production, while imports of "other agriculture" are for both purposes. The imports of non-food were calculated by first netting out agricultural imports from the import-share vector in the FAM. We then multiplied the revised import-share vector by the computed changes in outputs and incomes to derive the endogenous nonfood imports. Finally, we added to the endogenous non-food imports the imports by government and for investment, calculated as shares of the exogenous government and investment flows.

There are substantial food imports, despite large increases in domestic production. Total agricultural imports rise by 84 per cent, grain imports increase by 88 per cent, livestock imports rise by 73 per cent, and other-agriculture, which includes sorghum, rises by 83 per cent, due in large part to the greater share of livestock consumption. This, also, is consistent with international trends for semi-industrial countries, in which typically food-imports grow fast despite fast growth in agricultural production, because of rapid growth of urban output and urban populations and because of a shift to a more inefficient way of obtaining calories, through increased meat consumption.

The distributional consequences of the continuation of the bimodal strategy are much less favourable. The incomes of the poorest rural households (the agricultural workers and the campesinos) rise at a much slower rate than do urban incomes. Within the urban sector the incomes of workers rise at about the same rate as GDP while those of capitalists rise much faster. The result is an increase in inequality. The extrapolated functional distribution indicates a 13 per cent drop in the income-share of rural households and a 3 per cent increase in the ratio of the income-share of urban capitalists to urban workers.

Calorie consumption grows quite slowly, due both to population growth and to the fact that the marginal propensity to consume calories is substantially below unity. There is only a 6 per cent increase in percapita average daily calorie consumption for marginal urban workers, a 25 per cent increase in calorie consumption for agricultural workers, and a 28 per cent increase in calorie consumption for campesinos over the ten year period. In the absence of decreases in the relevant rates of population growth or of changes in development strategy, these rates of growth imply that the malnutrition of urban groups will continue with little abatement into the foreseeable future.

In sum, in our extrapolation the bimodal strategy has both favourable and unfavourable consequences. The growth results indicate rapid overall output and income growth, and the kinds of structural changes associated with the last phases of the transition to developed state in semi-industrial countries. There is also a slackening of inflationary pressures. On the negative side, the extrapolation of past policies and trends indicates a continued impoverishment of the agricultural sectors, increased reliance on food-imports, and an increase in inequality in the functional distribution of income. Due to rapid population growth, percapita income growth is slow, on the order of 1 per cent annually, and the nutritional status of vulnerable groups improves little.

In practice, the austerity program followed by Mexico in response to the debt crisis of the 1980s has produced a large trade surplus; however, this has been at the cost of very slow growth in overall income, a substantial decrease in per capita income, and a large increase in absolute poverty during this period. As we shall see below, the contrast between our equilibrium growth results and the actual performance of the Mexican economy between 1982 and 1986 has, in large part, been due to the choice of adjustment policies that have had disastrous impacts on growth and poverty.

In light of the mixed consequences of our bimodal-strategy extrapolations, it is worthwhile to explore whether the Mexican economy could do better by pursuing alternative strategies. Since it is the distributional consequences of the bimodal strategy which are most worrisome, the strategy alternatives we consider have mostly a distributional focus, though their implementation may (and does) have significant growth consequences as well.

The strategy alternatives we compare are: a unimodal agricultural strategy, which emphasizes the growth of a productive peasant-agriculture and reduces the traditional policy bias in favour of commercial farming; a populist strategy in the urban sectors, which is a high-wage, high-foodsubsidy strategy; and a wage-repression strategy, not unlike the one pursued since the debt crisis and fall in oil prices hit the Mexican economy. To enable comparison among strategies, all strategies are modelled as variants on the bimodal strategy. The projections of final demand changes and of world conditions are kept the same as in the bimodal "base," which becomes the reference point for all comparisons of strategies.

IV.2. THE UNIMODAL AGRICULTURAL STRATEGY

This strategy is intended to simulate the unimodal strategy of the Systema Alimentario Mexicano (SAM), adopted by the Mexican government during the brief period in which new oil discoveries and high oil prices generated a large increase in government receipts and in the availability of foreign exchange. This strategy attempted to retreat from the bimodal strategy in effect throughout most of Mexico's development, by reducing the bias in favour of commercial agriculture over small-scale agriculture in the allocation of credit, extension, inputs and public investment. As the reader will recall, the productivity results of the strategy were spectacular, but the strategy was in effect only between 1980 and 1982. It was quickly abandoned, once the fall in oil prices generated the severe budgetary and foreign exchange crisis which persists today.

The unimodal strategy was implemented in our model by transferring 25 per cent of value added in each of our three agricultural sectors to campesinos, and reducing the shares of commercial farmers and agricultural workers to compensate for the transfer. The reduction in share of agricultural workers simulates an unintended, but real, consequence of increased family farming: greater reliance on family labour at the expense of increased employment of hired labour. The increased emphasis on smallfarm production was assumed to require additional government investment. Government investment in agriculture was raised to a share corresponding to that in 1980-81, while the SAM strategy was in effect. This raised the share of agricultural investment in the government budget from 9 per cent to 15 per cent and amounted to a 20 000 million peso, or $4.6 billion, increase over the base government investment. The increased expenditure on agricultural infrastructure was allocated in the same share as in the construction sector between the purchase of final demand of construction (70 per cent) and the purchase of labour (30 per cent). The increased labour was assumed to be provided by agricultural labour, since the construction projects would occur in the countryside. This was modelled as an increase in government expenditure on agricultural labour. Finally, we assumed an increase in agricultural production of grains of 6 per cent, equal to that which occured between 1980 and 1982 but less than a third of the actual SAM-program increase between 1979 and 1982. (The actual results of the SAM strategy were too spectacular to extrapolate in their full glory for ten years!).

The growth consequences of the strategy are very favourable. The growth of GDP is the highest of any of the strategies we modelled. The unimodal strategy results in a level of GDP that is 323 billion 1980 pesos higher than in the bimodal strategy. The increase in grain production is 1.8 times that in the basic bimodal strategy. Net grain imports drop by about 4 billion compared to the bimodal strategy. Since GDP is considerably higher than in the bimodal strategy and livestock production increases by about 8 billion, this implies substantial import substitution in basic grains.

The consequences of the unimodal strategy for the government deficit are manageable, especially under high oil price conditions. Even though government expenditures increase by about 45 billion, government receipts increase substantially (31 billion), so that in the "base" unimodal strategy, the overall budgetary deficit increases by only 5.5 per cent and its share of GDP remains constant.

However, the balance of trade improves substantially, despite a large increase in non-food imports, because the increase in grain production induced by the implementation of the unimodal agricultural strategy converts Mexico from a large net grain importer into a grain exporter. The trade balance deficit drops to 18 per cent of exports, from 35 per cent under the bimodal strategy.

The income-distribution consequences favour small farmers, as they were intended to do. The relative share of this group is 40 per cent higher than with the bimodal strategy. The second-round multiplier effects thus favour small farmers as well. The improvement in the relative position of campesinos comes at the expense of urban groups: the share of urban workers and capitalists is 2 per cent lower and that of merchants and marginal workers is 1 per cent lower.

In absolute terms, however, all groups gain substantially from the unimodal strategy, both relative to the bimodal strategy and relative to 1980. The per capita incomes of campesinos are 46 per cent higher than with the bimodal strategy and 102 per cent higher than in 1980. Despite the reduced demand for agricultural labour due to the shift to family farming, the implementation of the public investment program raises the per capita income of agricultural workers by 1.2 per cent over the bimodal strategy. Relative to 1980, their per capita incomes increase by about 35 per cent. The per capita incomes of marginal workers improve very substantially (22 per cent) over 1980, as do those of urban workers (23 per cent). The percapita incomes of capitalists and merchants are also higher under the unimodal strategy than under the bimodal (by 2.8 and 4.1 per cent, respectively). Thus, even though there are relative losers from the strategy, unimodal agricultural development constitutes a

Pareto improvement over the bimodal strategy, since all groups gain substantially compared with the bimodal strategy.

Unimodal development leads to a substantial improvement in the nutritional status of the population as well. The total supply of calories is 50 per cent higher than with the bimodal strategy, and the nutritionally vulnerable groups'calorie consumption rises by 13 per cent over the basic strategy. Small farmers gain the most. Per-capita average daily calorie consumption by campesinos is 22 per cent higher than with the bimodal strategy, that of agricultural workers is 0.5 per cent higher and those of marginal urban workers and urban workers are 1.5 per cent and 0.5 per cent higher, respectively.

The results of the simulation of the SAM strategy thus indicate that the unimodal approach to Mexican agriculture offers a superior pattern of agricultural development to the present, bimodal one, from all points of view. The results of the unimodal strategy are an example of agricultural demand-led industrialization, or ADLI, advocated by Adelman (1984) for a context of low world demand for exports. The rationale for this strategy is:

1. Agriculture is much more labour-intensive than is even labourintensive manufacturing;

2. Increases in agricultural productivity generate increases in demand for the labour of the poorest of the poor, agricultural landless labour;

3. Increases in agricultural incomes generate high linkages into demand for labour-intensive manufactures on the consumption side and for manufactured inputs on the production side;

4. Expansion of agricultural production is less import-intensive than is an equivalent increase in manufacturing production;

5. Increases in agricultural output with good-practice, developing country technology are less capital intensive than increases in manufacturing; and finally

6. The agricultural infrastructure required to increase agricultural productivity (roads, irrigation, and drainage facilities) has a large employment effect.

The experiment results suggest that the abandonment of the unimodal strategy in 1982, in response to fiscal stringency and to the foreign exchange and debt crisis, was premature. The government-budget consequences of the strategy suggest that, after the brief transition period necessary to allow the induced income improvements to percolate through the economy, the government deficit increases very little and remains the same per cent of GDP as before. And there is substantial improvement in the balance of payments under the unimodal strategy, even in the absence of high world-prices for oil. When oil prices are high on world markets, the balance of trade deficit under the unimodal strategy drops from an already low 18 per cent to between 5 and 7 per cent of overall exports, depending on world grain price conditions.

IV.3. THE POPULIST STRATEGY

This strategy is the urban analogue of the unimodal strategy. The main elements of the strategy are an increase in wages and subsidies. We assume that the government raises minimum wages as well as the wages it pays its own employees and employees in government-owned enterprises and that this has the effect of raising all wages throughout the urban economy. It also increases subsidy rates on grains to urban consumers. This strategy was implemented in the model by: (1) raising the share of the wages of workers and marginals in value added by 25 per cent and reducing the share of capital-owners (government in petroleum and fertilizer and capitalists and merchants in the other sectors) to compensate; (2) increasing subsidy rates on grains to urban groups by 20 per cent; and (3) increasing the wages of government workers in the exogenous government-expenditure rows.

The assumed changes in the distribution of value added required recalculating the multiplier matrix for the populist strategy. Since wage earners spend a larger share of their income than capitalists and merchants, the new multiplier matrix has a larger effect. Since the consumption pattern of workers is different from that of capitalists, the effect is not uniform across sectors or income recipients.

To be fairly realistic, we also assumed that the increase in wages implied by the populist strategy has some output consequences in the private sector of the economy. To calculate output reductions due to increases in wages, we assumed constant elasticity of substitution production functions with elasticities that are less elastic than unity in agricultural processing (.8) and industry (.9) and more elastic in services (2.0) and commerce (3.0). We then adjusted the final demand vectors in these sectors so that, after the economy settles down from changes (1) through (3), the output levels in the affected sectors are reduced by the necessary amounts (3 per cent in agricultural processing, 12 per cent in industry, 8 per cent in services, and 4.3 per cent in commerce). In addition, we assumed that the populist strategy reduces the international competitiveness of Mexican exports, so that total Mexican exports are 8 per cent lower than they would be otherwise; this implies that demand for non-oil exports is elastic. Thus the overall design of the populist experiment allows for both positive and negative effects.

The results of this experiment are mostly compositional. Overall GDP is lower by 162 billion 1980 pesos. Nevertheless, the populist strategy produces a boom in the wage-goods producing sectors. The change in agricultural output is 6 per cent higher than under the bimodal strategy and the change in food processing output is 11 per cent higher. By the same token, there is a recession in the "luxury-goods" sectors. The change in non-food manufacturing is 5 per cent lower and the change in services plus commerce is 14 per cent lower than with the bimodal strategy.

On the income side, small farmers and agricultural workers are 2 per cent better off, and commercial farmers, who supply the bulk of the food for urban consumption, are 1.7 per cent better off than under the bimodal strategy. The main direct beneficiaries of the strategy, urban and marginal workers, are 8 per cent better off as a group than with the bimodal strategy. They thus retain about a third of their direct relative gains, once the output-reducing and expenditure-change effects work their way through the entire system. The main losers from the populist strategy are the capitalists, whose income is 17 per cent lower than with the base strategy. (Merchants are only 1 per cent worse off).

In per capita terms, all lower income groups are better off than with the bimodal strategy. Urban workers and urban marginal workers have about 8 per cent higher incomes, while campesino and agricultural workers are 2 per cent better off. The income improvements of the poor occur mainly at the expense of urban capitalists.

Not surprisingly, the populist strategy induces substantial macroeconomic imbalances. The government budget deficit rises substantially. Government receipts are 17 billion pesos lower than in the bimodal strategy and government expenditures are 81 billion higher. As a result, the total deficit is 38 per cent higher than with the bimodal strategy. The deficit rises to 5 per cent of GDP, suggesting that inflationary pressures under this strategy are very high.

However, under a regime of high oil prices, which substantially reduce the deficit, the ratio of the deficit to GDP would become 3.7 per cent. This is only slightly higher than in the base bimodal projection, suggesting that the populist strategy is likely to be a sustainable strategy over the long haul only under a high-price-of-oil regime.

The balance of trade consequences of the populist strategy are adverse as well, as might be expected. But the primary problem lies in the export rather than in the import performance of the economy. The shift in the distribution of income away from high-income groups with high import propensities reduces non-food imports by about 8 billion. At the same time, the shift in the income distribution towards wage earners and farmers improves the "efficiency" of the food system via a shift away from livestock and processed foods. It therefore reduces food imports very slightly (by about 4.5 per cent). As a result, overall imports are somewhat lower than in the bimodal solution. However, due to the loss in international competitiveness and due to lower production in manufacturing, services and commerce, non-oil exports are 12 per cent lower than in the bimodal strategy. The trade deficit rises to an ominous 42 per cent of exports. Even with high oil prices, the deficit continues to be a moderately high ratio to exports (between 27 and 23 per cent, depending on international grain prices).

The simulation results suggest that from a distributional perspective the strategy has substantial merit. However, it gives rise to severe imbalances in the government and trade deficits, suggesting severe inflationary pressures and a severe foreign-exchange crunch. Since Mexico actually implemented some version of the populist strategy during the highworld-price-of-oil era, the results of this simulation suggest that inflation and balance of payments problems would have plagued the Mexican economy even in the absence of a drop in oil revenues. Despite its distributional merits, the simulation results imply that, without high world prices for oil, the populist strategy is not a feasible one, at least at the level implemented, because of its macro-economic implications.

IV.4. THE WAGE REPRESSION STRATEGY

One of the ways Mexico has adjusted to the fiscal and foreign-exchange crunch since 1982 has been to shift to a wage repression strategy. This strategy consists of a typical IMF-inspired austerity program of cutting wages and subsidies, so as to reduce domestic absorption and thereby improve the balance of payments.

In our model, the strategy was implemented by imposing the reverse of all the changes made to simulate the populist strategy on the basic bimodal model. We reduced the share of wages in value-added, cut food subsidies to urban groups, and reduced the wages of government workers — all by the same proportions as in the populist strategy. We also assumed that the reduced wages have favourable output effects in the non-government manufacturing sectors, and we calculated the output increases with the same CES functions as in the populist strategy. We also assumed that Mexican exports are now more competitive on world markets.

The simulation results indicate that the wage-repression strategy is a disaster from all but a macro-balance point of view. Surprisingly, even though the magnitude of the share of value-added transferred away from workers in the wage-repression strategy is the same as the share of valueadded that had been added to workers in the populist strategy, the effects on the respective multiplier matrices are quantitatively very different. The wage-repression multiplier matrix has diagonal elements which are much smaller, and as a result, the second-round effects of exogenous injections are very small.

The wage-repression strategy accomplishes the objective of reducing the external macroeconmic disequilibrium of the economy. The trade balance turns from a substantial deficit to a small surplus. Imports plummet. In addition, because of an increase in competitiveness and a deficiency in domestic demand for food, exports increase dramatically. This experiment captures nicely the balance-of-payments impacts of austerity programs that cut domestic absorption in response to international financial disequilibria.

However, the budget deficit becomes very large as a result of the implementation of the wage-repression strategy, rising to 14 per cent of GDP from 3.6 per cent under the bimodal strategy. Government tax receipts are cut by 270 billion as a result of a general economic decline triggered by the wage-repression policies. Government expenditures are the lowest of any of the strategies, but they nevertheless decrease by substantially less than do government receipts. There is clearly a tradeoff between achieving internal and external balance with the wage-repression strategy.

In addition, the wage repression strategy is clearly a drastic remedy for achieving a balance of trade surplus. It results in a major depression, cutting GDP to 75 per cent of its 1980 value. All income groups suffer. But, somewhat surprisingly, the relative income drop that is the highest is for capitalists. For them, the indirect effects of the lower consumption of manufactured goods by wage earners more than negate the direct effects of the transfer of value added. Relatively, farmers do best, since the drastic drop in income shifts patterns of consumption to a higher share of food in overall expenditures.

The wage repression strategy is Pareto inferior for all groups in the economy, with very substantial per capita income drops relative to 1980. The drops in urban worker and marginal worker incomes are particularly severe, amounting to 44 per cent losses in per capita terms. Calorie consumption of vulnerable urban groups is cut very drastically relative to 1980, with drops of calorie consumption per capita ranging from 13 per cent for marginals and 7 per cent for other urban workers. Calorie consumption increases slightly for campesinos and for agricultural labour; however, these increases are only 83 per cent and 89 per cent, respectively, of the base, bimodal strategy. Mean per capita daily calorie consumption for marginal workers drops to 314 calories below the mean nutritional FAO minimum consumption norm of 2200 for an active life. Calorie decreases for vulnerable urban groups suggest that the implementation of the wage repression strategy is likely to lead to severe increases in malnutrition, morbidity and vulnerability to disease by large segments of the population.

Qualitatively, the simulation results parallel actual Mexican experience under the wage-repression strategy. Both in the experiment and in actuality, Mexico experiences a dramatic turnaround in its commodity trade deficit. However, this is at the cost of a substantial decline in per capita incomes, with urban groups being particularly hard-hit. It also comes at the cost of an increased internal fiscal disequilibrium. Quantitatively, the results of the policy experiment are more extreme, in part because the experiment is a ten-year extrapolation while the data available to reflect the actual performance of Mexico's economy under wage repression are for a four-year period (1982-1986). The urban groups, including urban capitalists and merchants, are hit particularly hard by the wage-repression strategy, as they were in actuality (Adelman and Taylor, 1989). The 5.3 per cent annual decline in per capita GNP in our experiment is more dramatic than the actual decline of 2.4 per cent annually between 1980 and 1986. On the trade side, Mexico's actual, remarkable turnaround in the commodity trade deficit produced a trade surplus of 380 billion pesos in 1986, which is double the surplus produced by the wage-repression experiment. The policy experiment generates a public-sector deficit that is 23 per cent larger than what actually occurred in 1986. These comparisons suggest that despite the economic disaster of the 1980s, Mexico achieved impressive structural changes at the macro level.

Comparison with the bimodal strategy under low-world-oil-price conditions like those that have led to the adoption of the wage-repression strategy indicates that continuation of the bimodal strategy would have had far superior income, output and inflation results. It also suggests that much of the current Mexican depression and inflation can be attributed to the choice of a wage-repression strategy as a method of adjusting to international financial disequilibria.

IV.5. IMPACT OF INTERNATIONAL PRICES

One of the major benefits of working with a quantitative model in policy analysis is that it permits counterfactual analysis. Up to now, we have focused the discussion on the impact of alternative development strategies implemented in the same world environment. We have made only passing references to the impact of world market conditions upon the outcomes of the strategies. We now turn to a discussion of the withinstrategy impact of different world-price regimes. We focus specifically on high and low world prices for petroleum and high and low world prices for basic grains. These give us four combinations of world-condition scenarios.

IV.5.1. The Design of the World Price Scenario Experiments

It is difficult to perform price experiments with a model that does not allow for substitution effects induced by changes in relative prices and changes in exchange rates. We do so by incorporating the major substitution effects on imports and exports and on domestic production exogenously into the model.

To calculate the effects on Mexican exports of alternative international prices for petroleum, we fitted regressions to data on Mexican oil and non-oil exports over the 1974-84 period. These regressions indicate that the elasticity of Mexican oil exports with respect to their price has been .039. There has also been a "Dutch-disease" phenomenon evident in Mexico's non-oil exports. When oil-prices increase by 1 per cent, non-oil exports are .24 per cent lower, due both to exchange-rate appreciation (the classical Dutch-disease phenomenon) and to the reduction in world growth rates that has been associated with higher petroleum prices.

Our estimate of the impact of world grain prices on domestic production is based on international cross-section studies. These suggest a medium-run production elasticity of about .2 for all basic grains taken together. (The production elasticities of individual crops are much higher, of course). The model then estimates the impact that the assumed changes in basic grain production would have on the imports and exports of basic grains.

Finally, to estimate the impact of world recession or world prosperity on remittances by Mexicans working in the United States (for which there are no time series and only vague estimates), we assumed that these vary in the same proportion as the ratio of United States income to Mexican income. A regression fitted to the ratio of U.S. income to Mexican income as a function of world oil prices and time indicates that the ratio of U.S. to Mexican income has an elasticity of .06 with respect to oil prices.

For the world price scenarios, we assumed a 50 per cent increase or decrease in the world price of oil or grain over the ten year period of our policy analysis. The oil price experiments therefore increase (decrease) oil exports by a factor of two when oil prices are high (low), and they reduce other exports by 12 per cent. Remittances are lowered (raised) by 30 per cent when oil prices are high (low).

In the design of the basic-grains price change experiments, we assumed that the government does not insulate producers from changes in the world price of grains, but that it does stabilize grain prices to urban consumers. In the grain-price experiments, we therefore assume a quantity response by domestic producers to changes in the world price of grain and a change in the amount of government grain subsidy to urban consumers. Specifically, when world prices for basic grains increase (decrease) by 50 per cent, we raised (lowered) domestic grain production by 12 per cent. These increases (decreases) in production go towards import substitution in grains. They are subtracted from the computed grain imports at the original marginal propensities to import basic grains, thereby de facto lowering (raising) these propensities. We also raised (lowered) government grain subsidies to urban consumers by increasing government payments to CONASUPO by 50 per cent when world prices of grain increase (decrease) by 50 per cent. The increased government subsidies are distributed as increased transfers to the various urban household categories in the same proportion as their expenditures on basic grains.

IV.5.2. World Price Scenario Simulation Results

It is apparent from Tables 9 through 14 that the best world environment for Mexico is one of high-oil, high-grain (HH) prices. High oil prices benefit Mexico because it is a petroleum exporter. And, even though Mexico is a grain importer, high grain prices are better because of the increased domestic grain production induced by higher world prices and because of the multiplier effects of increased grain production. The worst world environment is one of low-oil, low-grain (LL) prices like the present one. The other scenarios are in between. The high-oil low-grain (HL) price scenario is second best, while the low-oil high-grain (LH) price scenario is the second worst.

The discussion which follows focuses on the effect of world price scenarios under the bimodal strategy. But a glance at Tables 9 through 14 shows that the results are qualitatively similar for all strategies considered.

The impact of different world oil price regimes on overall GDP or on sectoral growth rates is noticeable but not dramatic, except in the petroleum sector itself. Comparing GDP in the high-oil price scenario with GDP in the low-oil price scenario, there is a difference of 294 billion pesos with high grain prices and 368 billion with low grain prices under the base bimodal strategy. With this 100 per cent swing in oil prices, GDP is only 4 per cent higher after ten years under the high-oil high-grain price (HH) scenario than under the low-oil high-grain price scenario (LH). The impact of different international price scenarios on household incomes is not very large either, especially in per capita terms. The largest beneficiaries from high oil prices are the capitalists, whose income is 6 per cent higher with high oil and high grain prices than it is with low-oil and high grain prices, and urban workers, whose income is 4 to 5 per cent higher. Commercial farmers benefit from high oil prices, by about 3 per cent. The incomes of all other groups are about one per cent higher under a high oil-price regime.

The grain price regime has noticeable effects on the incomes of rural groups, especially campesinos and agricultural workers. The per capita incomes of campesinos are 11 per cent higher in the HH solution than in the HL solution, and they are 5 per cent higher in the LH than in the LL solution.

The effects on agricultural workers are comparable. Urban groups benefit substantially as well from a high world price-of-grain regime, because the increased production and incomes in rural areas generate increased demand for urban products. The per capita incomes of urban workers are 8 per cent higher, those of capitalists are 11 per cent higher, those of merchants are 10 per cent higher, and those of marginal workers are 11 per cent higher under the HH as opposed to the HL solutions.

The nutritional status of both rural and urban groups is also higher in a high world grain-price environment, though by relatively less than their per capita incomes. The average number of calories consumed by nutritionally vulnerable groups is between 3 and 5 per cent higher when international prices for basic grains are high than when they are low (HH as compared to HL, in the bimodal solution) because the incomes of these groups are higher under these circumstances.

The primary effect of different world price regimes is on the overall degree of financial disequilibrium of the economy. The budget deficit is about 190 billion 1980 pesos lower when world oil prices are high than when they are low (HH versus LH, in the bimodal strategy), a difference of about two per centage points as a share of GDP. With high oil prices the trade deficit is about 70 billion pesos smaller when grain prices are high and 21 billion smaller when grain prices are low.

The grain price regime has a much smaller impact on the government budget deficit than it does on the trade deficit. The reduction in the budget deficit with high grain prices is on the order of 25 billion pesos. On the other hand, high grain prices reduce the trade deficit by about 63 billion pesos, mainly as a result of a dramatic drop in basic grain imports. They also affect the structure of imports. Low world grain prices increase the share of basic grain imports for human consumption dramatically (from a marginal share of about 52 per cent of agricultural imports to about 75 per cent). The share of non-food imports in total imports declines (from a marginal share of about 89 per cent to about 86 per cent of the change in imports). This is because the income distribution favours groups with high non-food import propensities when food prices are low. This is the opposite of agricultural demand-led industrialization (i.e., ADLI in reverse).

It is through the influence of different world price regimes on the budget and trade deficits that the world prices of petroleum and grain exercise their major impact on the Mexican economy. The magnitudes of the trade and the budget deficits, in turn, determine the extent of latitude for the adoption of different domestic development strategies. As a result, some domestic development strategies become more likely and others less likely.

Different world price scenarios loosen or tighten the limiting constraints on the choice of domestic development strategy. Thus, high oil prices make the adoption of a unimodal agricultural development strategy more feasible, by lowering both the trade and the budget deficits. Similarly, high world prices for petroleum convert an unsustainable budget deficit of 5.3 per cent of GDP under the populist strategy into a deficit of 3.7 per cent of GDP, and they convert the trade deficit from 42 per cent of exports to between 27 and 23 per cent of exports.

High oil prices therefore make consideration of the populist strategy more feasible from a macroeconomic point of view. The changes induced by world price conditions under the wage repression strategy are much smaller; as a result, even though the budget deficit improves under high grain-price conditions, it remains prohibitively large because of a very large drop in government tax revenues. But, as we saw, there are many other, more fundamental, reasons why the wage repression strategy is an undesirable one.

V.

CONCLUSION

Our analysis of the influence of different development strategies on production, incomes, nutrition, and income distribution in Mexico suggests that:

1. The continuation of the present bimodal agricultural strategy combined with the import-substitution policy of industrialization results in good overall growth performance but has adverse distributional consequences. There is a continued impoverishment of the agricultural sector and an increase of already high degrees of income inequality. In addition, high rates of population growth eat up the main fruits of high growth and lead to disappointing rates of growth of per capita income and per capita nutrition.

2. The unimodal strategy of agricultural development leads to a Pareto improvement over the bimodal strategy. Small farmers are the major beneficiaries of the unimodal strategy, but the incomes of all other groups are also substantially higher than under the bimodal strategy. There is some improvement in nutritional status, as well, and the distribution of income becomes somewhat more equal.

3. The populist strategy has favourable distributional and nutritional consequences, in both the urban and rural sectors. But the overall rate of growth of output is somewhat lower under a populist strategy, and in the absence of high oil prices the budget and trade deficits induced by this strategy make its adoption infeasible.

4. The wage-repression strategy has disastrous consequences for the growth of output, incomes, and the nutritional status of the population. There is a dramatic improvement in the trade deficit, but the budget deficit escalates to unmanageable proportions. The cost of achieving external balance with this strategy is therefore very high indeed.

5. The best world-price scenario for Mexico is one that combines high oil prices with high grain prices; the worst scenario is one that combines low oil prices with low grain prices. High oil prices raise the level of GDP by about 4 per cent above the low oil-price GDP in ten years, and high grain prices increase the level of GDP by about 1.5 per cent. But the primary effect of alternative world-price scenarios is on the twin balance-of-trade and government-budget deficits. These deficits affect the feasibility of alternative development strategies.

6. The major impact of the world price regime on the Mexican economy is through its effect on the choice of development strategy. A high world price of petroleum

facilitates the adoption of the unimodal strategy by loosening the constraints imposed by both deficits. In combination with high world prices for grain, high world prices for petroleum make the adoption of a unimodal strategy of agricultural development more likely. A low world price of petroleum makes the adoption of the disastrous wagerepression strategy more probable as a response to a binding balance of payments constraint. A high price of petroleum makes the adoption of the populist strategy more feasible.

Our experiments suggest that small-farmer strategies have a major role to play in achieving the dual objectives of growth and poverty alleviation in semi-industrialized developing countries. Our findings for Mexico in this regard mirror those of Adelman (1984) for Korea and Yeldan (1988) for Turkey. They highlight the advantages of Agricultural Demand-led Industrialization (ADLI), which consists of building a domestic massconsumption market by improving the productivity of agriculture and letting farmers share in the fruits of the improved productivity. Small- and medium-scale agriculture has larger linkages with domestic industry than does large-scale agriculture currently favoured by Mexican agricultural policy. Small farms are labour-intensive and use domestic implements and machinery. Small farmers' consumption patterns favour locally-produced goods and goods produced with more labour-intensive technologies. The first and second-round effects of increases in small-farmer incomes tend to have favourable macro effects, as well, both with regard to the foreign trade balance and with regard to the public-sector deficit, especially if they are accompanied by import substitution or export expansion in grains.

Successful agricultural development requires maintaining a delicate balance among productivity growth in the agricultural sector; the composition of output of the agricultural sector, especially between food grains and feed grains; and growth in urban incomes, which affect the level and composition of demand for food in the nonagricultural sector. Agricultural strategies can fail as an income-raising, poverty-reducing strategy in the medium run if the growth of agricultural productivity is too high relative to the rates of growth of the nonagricultural sectors plus growth in either agricultural import-substitution or agricultural exports. In the case of our unimodal development experiments for Mexico, the rate of growth of agricultural productivity exceeds that of urban incomes; however, grain imports are very high initially, so that import substitution in grains is able to absorb the difference.

How universal is the case for ADLI? The inherent short-run potential to achieve productivity gains in agriculture is likely to vary significantly among countries with different topographies and land densities, degrees of institutional responsiveness to market incentives in agriculture, size distributions of landholdings, and levels of rural education. De Janvry and Sadoulet (1987) provide general evidence concerning the changing relationships between agricultural growth, growth in overall GNP, and international trade in less-developed countries. Their estimates indicate that countries start with low growth in agriculture, relying on agricultural exports to fuel both industrialization and GNP growth. They then begin to industrialize and tend to neglect and tax agriculture. The result is that the slow growth in agricultural output becomes a binding constraint on industrial growth. At this point, most newly-industrializing developing countries start engaging in serious efforts to improve agricultural productivity. They then first go through an import-substitution phase (e.g., Korea) and, if they continue the agricultural strategy, they next move to a second agricultural-export phase (e.g., Indonesia and India). Then, with continued urban income growth, there is a shift in the composition of demand towards animal proteins. This, in turn, entails a vastly enhanced demand for feed grains and increased pressures for improvement in productivity of the agricultural sector. At this point, countries again turn to importing either feedgrains or foodgrains or both (e.g., Mexico). In the long run, therefore, the case for agricultural development appears strong, especially for newly industrializing countries and countries at the lowest levels of development.

NOTES

1. In 1969 Mexico had one of the most unequal distributions of income among the world's middle-income countries. For an international comparison of income inequality during the period see Adelman and Morris (1973).

2. The actual impact of SAM is difficult to quantify, due to inadequate data collection and unusually favourable weather conditions during 1981, the peak year of SAM. Regarding the spectacular performance of the basic grain sector during this period, however, there can be no disagreement. Andrade and Blanc (1987) note that basic grain production from 1980-1982 was far higher than in any other 3-year period in Mexico's history — including periods with similar sets of weather conditions. In the most serious effort to date to assess the production impacts and cost of SAM, these researchers also found strong indications that, even in its short lifetime, SAM was successful at stimulating basic food production on rainfed lands in small-farmers areas.

3. The government food budget includes government expenditures on all programmes and subprogrammes considered basic to the implementation of the SAM programme; see Andrade and Blanc (1987).

4. The effects of alternative structural adjustment strategies for Mexico in the 1980s are explored elsewhere (Adelman and Taylor, 1989).

REFERENCES

ADELMAN, I., "Beyond Export-led Growth." *World Development* 12: 973-986, 1984.

ADELMAN, I. and C.T. MORRIS, *Economic Growth and Social Equity in Developing Countries.* Stanford, Stanford University Press, 1973.

ADELMAN, I. and J.E. TAYLOR, "Is Structural Adjustment with a Human Face Possible? The Case of Mexico." University of California, Berkeley and Davis, Giannini Foundation Working Paper No. 500 (presented at the 1988 American Economics Association Meetings, New York, December 28-30), 1989.

ADELMAN, I., J.E. TAYLOR and S. VOGEL, "Life in a Mexican Village: A SAM Perspective." *Journal of Development Studies* (forthcoming), 1989.

ANDRADE, A. and N. BLANC, SAM's Cost and Impact on Production. In Austin and Esteva, eds., *Food Policy in Mexico — The Search for Self-Sufficiency.* Ithaca: Cornell University Press, 1987, pp. 215-248, 1987.

CENTRO NACIONAL DE INFORMACION Y ESTADISTICAS DEL TRABAJO (CENIET), "Analisis de Algunos Resultados de la Primera Encuesta de Trabajadores No Documentados Devueltos de los Estados Unidos." Mexico City: Mexican Secretaria del Trabajo y Prevision Social, 1978.

DE JANVRY, A. and E. SADOULET, "Agricultural Policy and General Equilibrium." *American Journal of Agricultural Economics* 69:230-246, 1987.

DEWALT, Billie R., "Mexico's Second Green Revolution: Food for Feed." *Mexican Studies/Estudios Mexicanos* 1(1), 1985.

GREENE, W.H., "Estimation of Limited Dependent Variable Models by Ordinary Least Squares and the Method of Moments." *Journal of Econometrics* 21:195-212, 1983.

GREENE, W.H., "On the Asymptotic Bias of the Ordinary Least Squares Estimator of the Tobit Model", *Econometrica* 49, 1981.

HEIEN, D., L.S. JARVIS and F. PERALI, "Food Consumption in Mexico: Demographic and Economic Effects." *Food Policy* (forthcoming), 1989.

KING, B., "What is a SAM? A Layman's Guide to Social Accounting Matrices." World Bank Staff Working Paper N°463, 1981.

LUSTIG, N., "Politica de precios y subsidios del SAM y distribucin del ingreso." Segundo Reporte, Colegio de Mexico SINE/SAM, 1982.

LUSTIG, N., "Distribucion del ingreso y consumo de alimentos: estructura, tendencias y requerimientos redistributivos a nivel regional." Demografia y Economia XVI(2):107-145, 1982.

PYATT, G. and J.I. ROUND, "Accounting and Fixed-price Multipliers in a Social Accounting Matrix Framework." *Economic Journal* 89:339-364.

STONE, R.A., "The Disaggregation of the Household Sector in the National Accounts." In G. Pyatt and J.I. Round, Social Accounting Matrices: A Basis for Planning. Washington, D.C.: *The World Bank,* 1985.

YELDAN, E., "Turkish Economy in Transition: A General Equilibrium Analysis of the Export-led Versus Domestic Demand-led Strategies of Development." Doctoral Dissertation, Applied Economics, University of Minnesota, 1988.

WHERE TO OBTAIN OECD PUBLICATIONS
OÙ OBTENIR LES PUBLICATIONS DE L'OCDE

Argentina – Argentine
Carlos Hirsch S.R.L.
Galeria Güemes, Florida 165, 4° Piso
1333 Buenos Aires
Tel. 30.7122, 331.1787 y 331.2391
Telegram: Hirsch–Baires
Telex: 21112 UAPE–AR. Ref. s/2901
Telefax:(1)331-1787

Australia – Australie
D.A. Book (Aust.) Pty. Ltd.
11–13 Station Street (P.O. Box 163)
Mitcham, Vic. 3132   Tel. (03)873.4411
Telex: AA37911 DA BOOK
Telefax: (03)873.5679

Austria – Autriche
OECD Publications and Information Centre
4 Simrockstrasse
5300 Bonn (Germany)   Tel. (0228)21.60.45
Telex: 8 86300 Bonn
Telefax: (0228)26.11.04
Gerold & Co.
Graben 31
Wien I   Tel. (0222)533.50.14

Belgium – Belgique
Jean De Lannoy
Avenue du Roi 202
B–1060 Bruxelles
Tel. (02)538.51.69/538.08.41
Telex: 63220 Telefax: (02)538.08.41

Canada
Renouf Publishing Company Ltd.
1294 Algoma Road
Ottawa, Ont. K1B 3W8 Tel. (613)741.4333
Telex: 053–4783 Telefax: (613)741.5439
Stores:
61 Sparks Street
Ottawa, Ont. K1P 5R1 Tel. (613)238.8985
211 Yonge Street
Toronto, Ont. M5B 1M4 Tel. (416)363.3171
Federal Publications
165 University Avenue
Toronto, ON M5H 3B9 Tel. (416)581.1552
Telefax: (416)581.1743
Les Publications Fédérales
1185 rue de l'Université
Montréal, PQ H3B 1R7 Tel.(514)954–1633
Les Éditions La Liberté Inc.
3020 Chemin Sainte-Foy
Sainte-Foy, P.Q. G1X 3V6
Tel. (418)658.3763
Telefax: (418)658.3763

Denmark – Danemark
Munksgaard Export and Subscription Service
35, Norre Sogade, P.O. Box 2148
DK–1016 Kobenhavn K
Tel. (45 33)12.85.70
Telex: 19431 MUNKS DK
Telefax: (45 33)12.93.87

Finland – Finlande
Akateeminen Kirjakauppa
Keskuskatu 1, P.O. Box 128
00100 Helsinki   Tel. (358 0)12141
Telex: 125080 Telefax: (358 0)121.4441

France
OECD/OCDE
Mail Orders/Commandes par correspondance:
2 rue André-Pascal
75775 Paris Cedex 16   Tel. (1)45.24.82.00
Bookshop/Librairie:
33, rue Octave-Feuillet
75016 Paris   Tel. (1)45.24.81.67
(1)45.24.81.81
Telex: 620 160 OCDE
Telefax: (33–1)45.24.85.00
Librairie de l'Université
12a, rue Nazareth
13602 Aix-en-Provence Tel. 42.26.18.08

Germany – Allemagne
OECD Publications and Information Centre
4 Simrockstrasse
5300 Bonn   Tel. (0228)21.60.45
Telex: 8 86300 Bonn
Telefax: (0228)26.11.04

Greece – Grèce
Librairie Kauffmann
28 rue du Stade
105 64 Athens   Tel. 322.21.60
Telex: 218187 LIKA Gr

Hong Kong
Government Information Services
Publications (Sales) Office
Information Service Department
No. 1 Battery Path
Central   Tel. (5)23.31.91
Telex: 802.61190

Iceland – Islande
Mal Mog Menning
Laugavegi 18, Postholf 392
121 Reykjavik   Tel. 15199/24240

India – Inde
Oxford Book and Stationery Co.
Scindia House
New Delhi 110001   Tel. 331.5896/5308
Telex: 31 61990 AM IN
Telefax: (11)332.5993
17 Park Street
Calcutta 700016   Tel. 240832

Indonesia – Indonésie
Pdii-Lipi
P.O. Box 269/JKSMG/88
Jakarta12790   Tel. 583467
Telex: 62 875

Ireland – Irlande
TDC Publishers – Library Suppliers
12 North Frederick Street
Dublin 1   Tel. 744835/749677
Telex: 33530 TDCP EI Telefax : 748416

Italy – Italie
Libreria Commissionaria Sansoni
Via Benedetto Fortini, 120/10
Casella Post. 552
50125 Firenze   Tel. (055)645415
Telex: 570466 Telefax: (39.55)641257
Via Bartolini 29
20155 Milano   Tel. 365083
La diffusione delle pubblicazioni OCSE viene
assicurata dalle principali librerie ed anche
da:
Editrice e Libreria Herder
Piazza Montecitorio 120
00186 Roma   Tel. 679.4628
Telex: NATEL I 621427
Libreria Hoepli
Via Hoepli 5
20121 Milano   Tel. 865446
Telex: 31.33.95 Telefax: (39.2)805.2886
Libreria Scientifica
Dott. Lucio de Biasio "Aeiou"
Via Meravigli 16
20123 Milano   Tel. 807679
Telefax: 800175

Japan– Japon
OECD Publications and Information Centre
Landic Akasaka Building
2–3–4 Akasaka, Minato-ku
Tokyo 107   Tel. 586.2016
Telefax: (81.3)584.7929

Korea – Corée
Kyobo Book Centre Co. Ltd.
P.O. Box 1658, Kwang Hwa Moon
Seoul   Tel. (REP)730.78.91
Telefax: 735.0030

**Malaysia/Singapore –
Malaisie/Singapour**
University of Malaya Co-operative Bookshop
Ltd.
P.O. Box 1127, Jalan Pantai Baru 59100
Kuala Lumpur
Malaysia   Tel. 756.5000/756.5425
Telefax: 757.3661
Information Publications Pte. Ltd.
Pei-Fu Industrial Building
24 New Industrial Road No. 02–06
Singapore 1953   Tel. 283.1786/283.1798
Telefax: 284.8875

Netherlands – Pays-Bas
SDU Uitgeverij
Christoffel Plantijnstraat 2
Postbus 20014
2500 EA's-Gravenhage Tel. (070)78.99.11
Voor bestellingen: Tel. (070)78.98.80
Telex: 32486 stdru Telefax: (070)47.63.51

New Zealand –Nouvelle-Zélande
Government Printing Office
Customer Services
P.O. Box 12–411
Freepost 10–050
Thorndon, Wellington
Tel. 0800 733–406 Telefax: 04 499–1733

Norway – Norvège
Narvesen Info Center – NIC
Bertrand Narvesens vei 2
P.O. Box 6125 Etterstad
0602 Oslo 6
Tel. (02)67.83.10/(02)68.40.20
Telex: 79668 NIC N Telefax: (47 2)68.53.47

Pakistan
Mirza Book Agency
65 Shahrah Quaid-E-Azam
Lahore 3   Tel. 66839
Telex: 44886 UBL PK. Attn: MIRZA BK

Portugal
Livraria Portugal
Rua do Carmo 70–74
1117 Lisboa Codex   Tel. 347.49.82/3/4/5

**Singapore/Malaysia
Singapour/Malaisie**
See "Malaysia/Singapore"
Voir "Malaisie/Singapour"

Spain – Espagne
Mundi-Prensa Libros S.A.
Castello 37, Apartado 1223
Madrid 28001   Tel. (91) 431.33.99
Telex: 49370 MPLI Telefax: (91) 275.39.98
Libreria Internacional AEDOS
Consejo de Ciento 391
08009 –Barcelona   Tel. (93) 301–86–15
Telefax: (93) 317–01–41

Sweden – Suède
Fritzes Fackboksföretaget
Box 16356, S 103 27 STH
Regeringsgatan 12
DS Stockholm   Tel. (08)23.89.00
Telex: 12387 Telefax: (08)20.50.21
Subscription Agency/Abonnements:
Wennergren-Williams AB
Box 30004
104 25 Stockholm   Tel. (08)54.12.00
Telex: 19937 Telefax: (08)50.82.86

Switzerland – Suisse
OECD Publications and Information Centre
4 Simrockstrasse
5300 Bonn (Germany)   Tel. (0228)21.60.45
Telex: 8 86300 Bonn
Telefax: (0228)26.11.04
Librairie Payot
6 rue Grenus
1211 Genève 11   Tel. (022)731.89.50
Telex: 28356
Maditec S.A.
Ch. des Palettes 4
1020 Renens/Lausanne Tel. (021)635.08.65
Telefax: (021)635.07.80
United Nations Bookshop/Librairie des Nations-Unies
Palais des Nations
1211 Genève 10
Tel. (022)734.60.11 (ext. 48.72)
Telex: 289696 (Attn: Sales)
Telefax: (022)733.98.79

Taïwan – Formose
Good Faith Worldwide Int'l. Co. Ltd.
9th Floor, No. 118, Sec. 2
Chung Hsiao E. Road
Taipei   Tel. 391.7396/391.7397
Telefax: (02) 394.9176

Thailand – Thalande
Suksit Siam Co. Ltd.
1715 Rama IV Road, Samyan
Bangkok 5   Tel. 251.1630

Turkey – Turquie
Kültur Yayinlari Is–Türk Ltd. Sti.
Atatürk Bulvari No. 191/Kat. 21
Kavaklidere/Ankara   Tel. 25.07.60
Dolmabahce Cad. No. 29
Besiktas/Istanbul   Tel. 160.71.88
Telex: 43482B

United Kingdom – Royaume-Uni
H.M. Stationery Office
Gen. enquiries   Tel. (01) 873 0011
Postal orders only:
P.O. Box 276, London SW8 5DT
Personal Callers HMSO Bookshop
49 High Holborn, London WC1V 6HB
Telex: 297138 Telefax: 873.8463
Branches at: Belfast, Birmingham, Bristol,
Edinburgh, Manchester

United States – États-Unis
OECD Publications and Information Centre
2001 L Street N.W., Suite 700
Washington, D.C. 20036–4095
Tel. (202)785.6323
Telex: 440245 WASHINGTON D.C.
Telefax: (202)785.0350

Venezuela
Libreria del Este
Avda F. Miranda 52, Aptdo. 60337
Edificio Galipan
Caracas 106
Tel. 951.1705/951.2307/951.1297
Telegram: Libreste Caracas

Yugoslavia – Yougoslavie
Jugoslovenska Knjiga
Knez Mihajlova 2, P.O. Box 36
Beograd   Tel. 621.992
Telex: 12466 jk bgd

Orders and inquiries from countries where
Distributors have not yet been appointed
should be sent to: OECD Publications
Service, 2 rue André-Pascal, 75775 Paris
Cedex 16.
Les commandes provenant de pays où
l'OCDE n'a pas encore désigné de distributeur devraient être adressées à : OCDE,
Service des Publications, 2, rue André-
Pascal, 75775 Paris Cedex 16.

OECD PUBLICATIONS, 2 rue André-Pascal, 75775 PARIS CEDEX 16
PRINTED IN FRANCE
(41 89 08 1) ISBN 92-64-13369-0 - No. 44971 1990